D1304658

A Taste of the Good Life

At the Heart of this Book

Nashville is home of Saint Thomas Heart Institute, one of the top five programs in the nation in cardiac treatment. That means we all have a deep and continuing interest in good heart health.

For years we've been showing cardiac rehabilitation patients there are many good-tasting foods that are also good for you. We have done this through the Saint Thomas Heart Institute Heart Healthy Cooking Schools and our first cookbook, *A Taste of the Good Life from the Heart of Tennessee*. In that book, we took some "not so good for you" down-home cooking favorites and transformed the recipes into low-fat, low-cholesterol southern meals.

Now we'd like to share some heart healthy recipes from across the world. Transport yourself over the ocean to the region known as the Mediterranean, where people live longer and healthier lives. In this cookbook, we'll explore the Mediterranean lifestyle, which not only includes certain foods, beverages, and methods of cooking, but also relaxation and physical activity. Throughout the cookbook, you'll find tasty traditional dishes and helpful tips on exercise and leading an active lifestyle.

All of our recipes have been carefully analyzed to make sure they fall within American Heart Association guidelines for low-fat, low-cholesterol cooking. At the end of each recipe, we've given you the nutritional information you need to keep track of your intake of fat, calories, and sodium.

Proceeds from the sale of this book will be used to fund the Cardiac Health and Rehabilitation Department's Patient Education Fund, teaching others to live long, healthy lives.

We hope you enjoy learning more about the Mediterranean lifestyle.

E. Dale Batchelor M.D.

E. Dale Batchelor, M.D.
Saint Thomas Hospital

A Taste of the Good Life
from the Heart of the Mediterranean

John Guider Studio specializes in art and commercial photography. Guider has traveled and photographed extensively in the Mediterranean region, where the interior shots were taken. Since opening his doors in 1974, he has built a very extensive resume that includes a long list of awards and achievements. Guider is also active in the Nashville area, donating artwork and professional services to schools and organizations.

A Taste of the Good Life
From the Heart of the Mediterranean

Project Manager: Greg Palevo, M.Sc.
Recipe and Menu Editor: Kitty Fawaz, R.D., L.D.N.
Contributing Editor: Sunny Thompson, R.D., L.D.N.
Essayists: Samantha Owens, Susan Morgenstern
Typists: Connie Rafalowski, Lucille Nabors
Food Stylist: Teresa Blackburn
Project Advisor: Sharon Blandford

This cookbook is a collection of favorite recipes,
which are not necessarily original recipes.

Published by Saint Thomas Health Services

Copyright © 2003 by
Saint Thomas Health Services
4220 Harding Road
Nashville, Tennessee 37205
(615) 222-2008

Library of Congress Catalog Number: 2002096622
ISBN: 0-9655243-1-0

Edited, Designed, and Manufactured by
Favorite Recipes® Press
an imprint of

FRP

P.O. Box 305142
Nashville, Tennessee 37230
(800) 358-0560

Project Editor: Debbie Van Mol, R.D.
Art Director: Steve Newman

Manufactured in the United States
First Printing: 2003
7,500 copies

Additional copies of *A Taste of the Good Life*, and other information on Saint Thomas programs, may be obtained by calling (800) 222-3541, or by writing to Saint Thomas Health Services, 4220 Harding Road, Nashville, Tennessee, 37205.

Contents

The Heart of the Mediterranean Diet

People who live in the sixteen countries bordering the Mediterranean Sea experience a decreased risk and incidence of cardiovascular disease and certain cancers. Death rates from heart disease are one-half to one-third less than in the United States. Also, according to the Lyon Diet Heart Study, the Mediterranean diet showed a 76 percent reduction in heart attacks and related complications compared to the dietary guidelines of the American Heart Association.

So what is the Mediterranean diet? There's nothing magical about the food and there is no single cuisine for the regions that border the Mediterranean Sea. People of the Mediterranean area owe their good health to eating plenty of grains, ample amounts of fruits and vegetables (eaten raw or prepared using nutrient-saving cooking techniques), legumes (beans and peas) and some nuts, using olive oil as their primary source of fat, eating less red meat and poultry, and eating more fish.

Since fresh milk is not readily available, yogurt and cheese are eaten regularly. Wine consumed in moderation with meals is an option. Overall, the diet is low in saturated fat and animal protein, and high in monounsaturated fat, omega-3 fatty acids, carbohydrates, fiber, antioxidant nutrients, and phytochemicals.

Be aware the components of the Mediterranean lifestyle go beyond food. Traditionally, the people of this region are physically active and maintain a lean body weight, which also plays a role in disease prevention. Mealtime provides a high degree of social support, as family members and friends are involved in preparing, sharing, and enjoying meals. They have lengthy meals that provide time for relaxation and after-lunch siestas that offer relief from daily stress.

In fact, the "heart" of the Mediterranean diet may actually be an overall lifestyle that lends itself to cardiovascular health.

MEDITERRANEAN
DIET

MEDITERRANEAN DIET PYRAMID

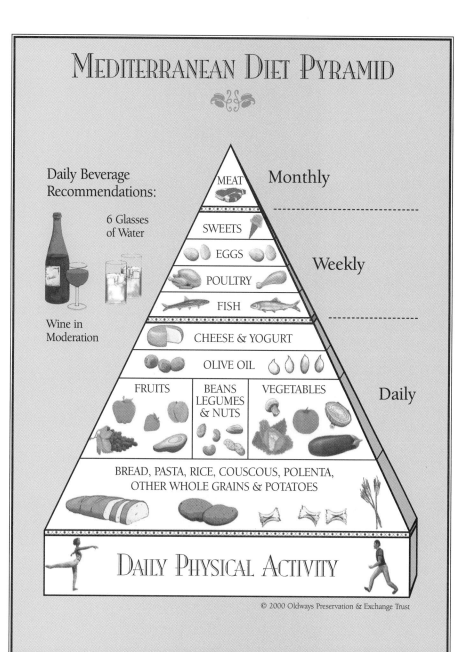

Daily Beverage Recommendations:

6 Glasses of Water

Wine in Moderation

Monthly

MEAT

- - - - - - - - - - - - - - - - - - - -

SWEETS

EGGS

Weekly

POULTRY

FISH

- - - - - - - - - - - - - - - - - - - -

CHEESE & YOGURT

OLIVE OIL

FRUITS | BEANS LEGUMES & NUTS | VEGETABLES

Daily

BREAD, PASTA, RICE, COUSCOUS, POLENTA, OTHER WHOLE GRAINS & POTATOES

DAILY PHYSICAL ACTIVITY

If you're interested in modifying your eating style, you're in luck.
The key elements of the Mediterranean diet are easily accessible here in the United States. Refer to the Mediterranean Diet Pyramid for guidance in selecting your intake of these foods. Try these tips to get started:

Make foods such as pasta, bread, and cereals, including plenty of whole grains, the cornerstone of your diet.

Eat generous amounts of vegetables and fruits.

Include more beans and other legumes in your diet as you cut down on meat.

Let olive oil be your primary fat source, and keep overall fat intake to a minimum to maintain a low-fat diet.

MEDITERRANEAN DIET PYRAMID

Now That You're Eating and Cooking Right...

A heart healthy lifestyle involves more than food: Exercise is at the top of the priority list.

The people of the Mediterranean get a lot of exercise. In these countries, the busy streets are filled with bicycles and walkers.

Exercising regularly is a major component of staying healthy and increases the total number of calories your body burns each day. This includes pleasurable activities such as gardening, cycling, walking, and swimming.

Understanding your metabolism plays a big part in weight gain and loss. Your resting metabolic rate (RMR) is the number of calories you burn at rest, and this will explain just how much you can eat per day. If your RMR is high, you can eat more than most and will not gain weight. If your RMR is low, you have the body type that even when active, a small amount of calories are hard to burn off.

Your RMR depends on your gender, age, body composition, and genetics. Men generally burn more calories than women. They tend to have higher muscle content, and muscle burns more calories. Regular exercise and strength training will build your muscle content, boosting your overall metabolic rate.

How much should you weigh? An easy way to determine a healthy weight is by using the Body Mass Index (BMI), a simple calculation that compares your height to your weight.

For men, the desirable BMI is 22 to 24, and for women, 21 to 23. Above 27 is considered overweight, and increases your risk of heart disease, diabetes, and other lifestyle-related diseases. Take a look at the BMI chart on Page 9 to see how you measure up.

Body Mass Index (BMI) Risk Levels (for adults)

Height	Minimal Risk (BMI under 25)	Moderate Risk (BMI 25–29.9) Overweight	High Risk (BMI 30 and above) Obese
4' 10"	118 lbs. or less	119–142 lbs.	143 lbs. or more
4' 11"	123 or less	124–147	148 or more
5' 0"	127 or less	128–152	153 or more
5' 1"	131 or less	132–157	158 or more
5' 2"	135 or less	136–163	164 or more
5' 3"	140 or less	141–168	169 or more
5' 4"	144 or less	145–173	174 or more
5' 5"	149 or less	150–179	180 or more
5' 6"	154 or less	155–185	186 or more
5' 7"	158 or less	159–190	191 or more
5' 8"	163 or less	164–196	197 or more
5' 9"	168 or less	169–202	203 or more
5' 10"	173 or less	174–208	209 or more
5' 11"	178 or less	179–214	215 or more
6' 0"	183 or less	184–220	221 or more
6' 1"	188 or less	189–226	227 or more
6' 2"	193 or less	194–232	233 or more
6' 3"	199 or less	200–239	240 or more
6' 4"	204 or less	205–245	246 or more

(Adapted from *Obesity Education Initiative: Clinical Guidelines on the Identification, Evaluation, and Treatment of Overweight and Obesity in Adults*, National Institutes of Health, National Heart, Lung, and Blood Institute. Preprint June 1998)

BODY MASS INDEX

CELEBRATIONS AND SEASONS

Holidays and traditions vary in cultures across the globe. In Spain, for example, because of the great difference in climate within the country, customs are completely different from one region to another. Spaniards from the northern regions decorate their homes with mistletoe and holly, while those in the southern regions decorate with geraniums and heliotrope.

And just as decorations differ, Spanish cuisine differs from region to region. For instance, each region has its own special way of preparing paella, the saffron-flavored rice dish that is one of the mainstays of their cooking.

In much of Spain, however, the traditional Christmas Eve dinner is the same. It consists of seafood, almond soup, roasted capon or turkey stuffed with truffles, broiled sea bream with potatoes, red cabbage, dried fruit and nuts, along with a wide assortment of sweets. This meal, as well as dinner on Christmas Day, is a leisurely celebration shared with immediate and extended family.

The luscious holiday and seasonal recipes here could be healthy—and heartily enjoyed—additions to your family's traditions.

CHRISTMAS EVE DINNER IN SPAIN

Garlic Shrimp

Castilian Garlic Soup *page 13* ♦ Almond Soup

Snapper in Parsley Sauce *page 14* ♦ Roasted Capon

Roasted Potatoes ♦ Red Cabbage

Dried Fruit and Nuts

Flan *page 168* ♦ Almond Squares ♦ Grape Tart *page 15*

GARLIC SHRIMP

1 pound medium shrimp
1 tablespoon olive oil ♦ 3 garlic cloves, minced
1 bay leaf ♦ 1/4 teaspoon crushed red pepper
1/8 teaspoon salt ♦ 2 tablespoons dry white wine
2 tablespoons fresh lemon juice
2 tablespoons chopped fresh parsley

Peel and devein the shrimp, leaving the tails intact. Combine the olive oil, garlic, bay leaf and red pepper in a large nonstick skillet. Cook over high heat for 30 seconds or just until the garlic begins to color, stirring constantly. Stir in the shrimp and salt. Cook for 2 to 3 minutes or until the shrimp turn pink, stirring constantly. Stir in the wine and lemon juice. Discard the bay leaf. Remove the shrimp to a serving platter and sprinkle with the parsley. Serve immediately. **Yield:** 8 appetizer servings.

PER SERVING:
CALORIES: 80; CARBOHYDRATE: 1 g; PROTEIN: 12 g; TOTAL FAT: 3 g;
CHOLESTEROL: 87 mg; SODIUM: 85 mg; FIBER: 0 g;
CALORIES FROM FAT: 34%

Castilian Garlic Soup
(Sopa de Ajo Castellana)

2 teaspoons extra-virgin olive oil
8 (or more) garlic cloves ♦ 1 teaspoon paprika
1/4 teaspoon cayenne pepper or black pepper
1 (16-ounce) can fat-free less-sodium chicken broth
4 teaspoons sodium-free chicken bouillon granules
4 cups hot water ♦ 1/4 teaspoon cumin
1/8 teaspoon crumbled saffron threads or turmeric
4 (1/2-inch-thick) slices crusty bread ♦ 4 eggs (optional)
2 tablespoons freshly grated Parmigiano-Reggiano or
Parmesan cheese

Spray a large saucepan with nonstick cooking spray. Heat the olive oil in the prepared saucepan over medium heat. Sauté the garlic in the oil for 10 to 15 minutes or until golden brown. Remove the garlic to a small bowl. Remove the saucepan from the heat and stir in the paprika and cayenne pepper. Add the broth, bouillon and hot water and mix well. Cook until the bouillon granules dissolve, stirring frequently. Stir in the cumin and saffron. Mash the garlic with a fork and add to the bouillon mixture. Simmer, covered, for 15 to 20 minutes, stirring occasionally.

Arrange the bread slices in a single layer on a baking sheet. Broil until brown on both sides, turning once. Poach the eggs 1 at a time in the simmering soup, stirring the soup to make a whirlpool into which you drop the egg. Poach until the white is firm and encloses the egg, or to the desired degree of doneness. Ladle the soup into 4 ovenproof soup bowls, placing 1 egg in each bowl. Top each serving with a slice of toasted bread and sprinkle with the cheese. Arrange the bowls on a baking sheet. Broil until the cheese melts. The addition of the eggs will add 75 calories, 6.2 grams of protein, 5 grams of fat, 213 milligrams of cholesterol and 63 milligrams of sodium to each serving. **Yield:** 4 servings.

Per Serving:
Calories: 140; Carbohydrate: 19.4 g; Protein: 5.2 g; Total Fat: 4.2 g; Cholesterol: 4.5 mg; Sodium: 385 mg; Fiber: 0.7 g; Calories from Fat: 27%

Garlic soup was originally a peasant dish originating in the high central plains of Spain. It is traditionally flavored with warm roasted garlic and homemade chicken stock. Spanish cooks sometimes poach an egg in the soup for each serving. Serve the soup in ovenproof soup bowls; earthenware bowls are traditionally used in Spain.

Celebrations and Seasons

SNAPPER IN PARSLEY SAUCE
(PARGO CON SALSA DE PEREJIL)

4 (6-ounce) red snapper fillets or
firm white fish fillets
2 cups fresh parsley leaves
1 cup chopped onion
1/2 cup clam juice
2 tablespoons fresh lime juice
1/4 teaspoon salt
3 garlic cloves

Arrange the fillets in a 9×13-inch baking dish sprayed with nonstick cooking spray. Process the parsley leaves, onion, clam juice, lime juice, salt and garlic in a blender or food processor until smooth and pour over the fillets.

Bake at 400 degrees for 18 minutes or until the fillets flake easily when tested with a fork. **Yield:** 4 servings.

PER SERVING:
CALORIES: 147; CARBOHYDRATE: 6.8 g; PROTEIN: 25.2 g; TOTAL FAT: 1.9 g;
CHOLESTEROL: 43 mg; SODIUM: 286 mg; FIBER: 1.8 g;
CALORIES FROM FAT: 12%

CELEBRATIONS
AND SEASONS

GRAPE TART

Crust

1 cup flour ♦ ¼ cup yellow cornmeal ♦ 3 tablespoons sugar
½ teaspoon baking powder ♦ ½ teaspoon salt
¼ cup (½ stick) margarine, chilled and cut into small pieces
3 tablespoons orange juice ♦ 1 teaspoon flour

Grape Filling and Assembly

2¼ cups seedless red grapes ♦ 2¼ cups seedless black grapes
2 tablespoons granulated sugar ♦ 1 tablespoon cornstarch
¾ teaspoon vanilla extract ♦ ¼ teaspoon cinnamon
1 teaspoon water ♦ 1 egg yolk ♦ 1 teaspoon turbinado sugar (optional)

For the crust, combine 1 cup flour, cornmeal, sugar, baking powder and salt in a food processor. Pulse 4 times or until blended. Add the margarine. Pulse 6 times or until crumbly. Add the orange juice gradually, processing constantly just until blended; do not allow the dough to form a ball. Pat the dough into a 4-inch round on plastic wrap. Chill, covered, for 15 minutes. Slightly overlap 2 sheets of plastic wrap on a damp surface. Place the chilled dough in the center of the plastic wrap. Cover the dough with 2 additional sheets of plastic wrap slightly overlapping. Roll the covered dough into an 11-inch round. Discard the top sheets of plastic wrap. Arrange the dough plastic wrap side up on a baking sheet lined with baking parchment. Discard the plastic wrap. Sprinkle with 1 teaspoon flour.

For the filling, combine the grapes, granulated sugar, cornstarch and vanilla in a bowl and mix gently. Spoon the grape mixture into the center of the round and spread to within 2 inches of the edge. Fold the edge of the dough toward the center, pressing gently to seal; the dough will only partially cover the grape mixture. Whisk the water and egg yolk in a bowl. Brush the egg wash over the edge of the dough. Sprinkle the turbinado sugar over the grape mixture and dough. Bake at 400 degrees for 25 minutes or until the crust is brown. Cut into 8 wedges. Serve warm or at room temperature. **Yield:** 8 (1-wedge) servings.

PER SERVING:
CALORIES: 231; CARBOHYDRATE: 40.8 g; PROTEIN: 2.9 g; TOTAL FAT: 6.7 g;
CHOLESTEROL: 27 mg; SODIUM: 180 mg; FIBER: 1.5 g;
CALORIES FROM FAT: 26%

CELEBRATIONS
AND SEASONS

MIDDLE EASTERN BUFFET

Baba Ghanouj

6 (6-inch) pita rounds, split
2 (1-pound) eggplant, cut horizontally into halves
1 or 2 garlic cloves
1/4 cup tahini (sesame seed paste)
3 tablespoons fresh lemon juice
1/2 teaspoon salt
1/8 teaspoon paprika
1 tablespoon chopped fresh parsley
1 teaspoon olive oil

Cut each pita half into 4 wedges. Arrange the wedges in a single layer on a baking sheet. Toast at 400 degrees for 9 minutes or until brown and crisp. Arrange the eggplant halves cut side down on a grill rack sprayed with nonstick cooking spray. Grill with the lid down over medium-hot coals (350 to 400 degrees) for 20 minutes or until tender. Cool slightly and peel the eggplant. Process the garlic in a food processor just until minced. Add the eggplant, tahini, lemon juice and salt. Process for 45 seconds or until smooth, scraping the side of the bowl once. Spoon the dip into a bowl. Chill, covered, in the refrigerator. Sprinkle with the paprika and parsley and drizzle with the olive oil just before serving. Serve with the pita wedges. **Yield:** 24 (2 tablespoons dip and 2 pita chips) servings.

Per Serving:
Calories: 74; Carbohydrate: 12.4 g; Protein: 2.4 g; Total Fat: 1.8 g;
Cholesterol: 0 mg; Sodium: 143 mg; Fiber: 1.6 g;
Calories from Fat: 22%

Celebrations
and Seasons

Stuffed Grape Leaves
(Dolmas)

Yogurt Sauce
1 cup plain low-fat yogurt ◆ 2 tablespoons chopped fresh mint
1 teaspoon grated lemon zest ◆ 1 teaspoon honey

Filling and Assembly
1³/4 cups finely chopped onions ◆ 1 tablespoon olive oil
1 garlic clove, minced ◆ 2 cups hot cooked long grain rice
1 (15-ounce) can no-salt-added chick-peas or garbanzo beans,
rinsed and drained
1/2 cup currants ◆ 1/3 cup pine nuts, toasted
2 tablespoons fresh lemon juice
1 tablespoon chopped fresh dill weed, or 1 teaspoon dried dill weed
1/4 teaspoon salt ◆ 1/4 teaspoon pepper
30 bottled large grape leaves ◆ 2 tablespoons fresh lemon juice

For the sauce, combine the yogurt, mint, lemon zest and honey in a bowl and mix well. Chill, covered, in the refrigerator.

For the filling, sauté the onions in the olive oil in a nonstick skillet over medium-high heat for 3 minutes or until tender. Stir in the garlic. Sauté for 1 minute. Remove from the heat. Stir in the rice, chick-peas, currants, pine nuts, 2 tablespoons lemon juice, dill weed, salt and pepper. Rinse the grape leaves with cold water; drain and pat dry. Discard the stems. Spoon 1 rounded tablespoon of the rice mixture into the center of each grape leaf. Bring 2 opposite points of each leaf to the center and fold over the filling; roll tightly as for a jelly roll. Arrange the stuffed grape leaves seam side down in a 9×13-inch baking dish sprayed with nonstick cooking spray. Drizzle with 2 tablespoons lemon juice. Bake, covered, at 350 degrees for 30 minutes or until heated through. Serve warm or chilled with the sauce.
Yield: 30 (1 stuffed grape leaf and 1¹/2 teaspoons sauce) servings.

Per Serving:
Calories: 60; Carbohydrate: 9.6 g; Protein: 1.8 g; Total Fat: 1.9 g;
Cholesterol: 0 mg; Sodium: 185 mg; Fiber: 1.6 g;
Calories from Fat: 29%

Rosemary Rack of Lamb

1 (1½-pound) French-cut lean rack of lamb (8 ribs)
3 tablespoons balsamic vinegar
1 tablespoon chopped fresh rosemary, or 1 teaspoon dried rosemary
2 garlic cloves, minced ♦ ⅛ teaspoon pepper
¼ cup fresh bread crumbs ♦ ¼ cup minced shallots
¼ cup dry white wine ♦ ½ cup low-salt chicken broth
2 teaspoons honey ♦ ½ teaspoon cornstarch
Sprigs of fresh thyme (optional) ♦ Red grapes (optional)

Trim the fat from the lamb. Combine the vinegar, 2 teaspoons of the fresh rosemary and garlic in a large sealable plastic bag. Add the lamb and seal tightly. Shake to coat. Marinate in the refrigerator for 6 to 12 hours, turning occasionally. Remove the lamb, reserving the marinade. Sprinkle the lamb with the pepper. Toss the bread crumbs and remaining 1 teaspoon fresh rosemary in a bowl. Pat the crumb mixture over the meaty side of the lamb. Arrange the lamb crumb side up on a baking sheet sprayed with nonstick cooking spray. Insert a meat thermometer into the thickest part of the lamb; do not allow the thermometer to touch bone. Bake at 450 degrees for 20 minutes or until the thermometer registers 145 degrees for medium-rare or to the desired degree of doneness.

Heat a large nonstick skillet sprayed with nonstick cooking spray over medium-high heat. Sauté the shallots in the hot skillet for 4 minutes. Stir in the wine and reserved marinade. Bring to a boil, stirring occasionally; reduce the heat. Simmer for 8 minutes or until the liquid evaporates, stirring occasionally. Stir in the broth. Bring to a boil; reduce the heat. Simmer for 5 minutes or until the mixture is reduced to ⅓ cup, stirring occasionally. Mix the honey and cornstarch in a small bowl and stir into the broth mixture. Bring to a boil. Boil for 1 minute or until slightly thickened and the consistency of a sauce, stirring constantly. Slice the rack into 8 chops and arrange on a serving platter. Garnish with thyme and grapes. Serve with the wine sauce. **Yield:** 4 (2 lamb chops and 2 teaspoons sauce) servings.

PER SERVING:
CALORIES: 208; CARBOHYDRATE: 7.7 g; PROTEIN: 20.6 g; TOTAL FAT: 9.7 g;
CHOLESTEROL: 65 mg; SODIUM: 87 mg; FIBER: 0.2 g;
CALORIES FROM FAT: 42%

Coat cuts of lamb, beef, chicken or pork with Sage, Parsley and Mint Herb Crust. Mix ½ teaspoon finely chopped garlic (optional), 2 tablespoons each chopped fresh sage and parsley, 1 teaspoon chopped fresh mint, 1 teaspoon orange zest, ½ teaspoon ground sea salt and 1 teaspoon coarsely ground pepper in a bowl. Cover the bottom of a dish with the herb mixture. Lightly brush the desired cut of meat with 1 tablespoon olive oil and then generously coat all sides with the herb mixture. Roast, sear or grill as desired.

Celebrations and Seasons

Mediterranean Chicken

12 garlic cloves
1/8 teaspoon salt
Juice of 1 lemon
1/4 teaspoon salt
6 boneless skinless chicken breasts
1 medium onion, vertically sliced
1/2 cup water
Pepper to taste

Mash the garlic and 1/8 teaspoon salt using a mortar and pestle. Combine the garlic mixture, lemon juice and 1/4 teaspoon salt in a bowl and mix well. Rub the chicken with the garlic mixture. Arrange the chicken in a single layer in a baking dish sprayed with nonstick cooking spray. Marinate, covered, in the refrigerator for 1 to 2 hours. Top with the onion. Spray the onion and chicken mixture with nonstick cooking spray. Pour the water over the chicken and season with pepper. Bake, covered with foil, at 375 degrees for 40 minutes or until the chicken is cooked through. **Yield:** 6 servings.

Per Serving:
Calories: 158; Carbohydrate: 3.8 g; Protein: 27.4 g; Total Fat: 3.2 g;
Cholesterol: 73 mg; Sodium: 209 mg; Fiber: trace;
Calories from Fat: 18%

Middle Eastern Rice

2 teaspoons olive oil
1 1/2 cups chopped onions
4 garlic cloves, minced
5 cups hot cooked rice
1/2 cup golden raisins
1/3 cup chopped fresh parsley
1/3 cup pine nuts, toasted
1/4 teaspoon pepper
1/8 teaspoon salt
Sprigs of fresh parsley (optional)

Heat the olive oil in a large nonstick skillet over medium heat. Sauté the onions and garlic in the hot oil for 3 minutes or until the onions are tender. Combine the onion mixture, rice, raisins, parsley, pine nuts, pepper and salt in a bowl and mix well. Garnish with parsley. Cook the rice using package directions omitting the fat and salt and substituting fat-free low-sodium chicken broth for the liquid. **Yield:** 6 (1-cup) servings.

Per Serving:
Calories: 327; Carbohydrate: 58 g; Protein: 5.9 g; Total Fat: 9.3 g;
Cholesterol: 0 mg; Sodium: 64 mg; Fiber: 2.2 g;
Calories from Fat: 25%

Celebrations
and Seasons

TABOULEH

6 cups fresh parsley, finely chopped
3 Roma tomatoes, finely chopped
1/2 cup finely chopped green onions
1/2 cup fresh mint, finely chopped
1/4 cup bulgur
1/4 cup lemon juice, or to taste
1 tablespoon olive oil
1/8 teaspoon salt
Pepper to taste

Combine the parsley, tomatoes, green onions, mint, bulgur, lemon juice, olive oil, salt and pepper in a bowl and mix well. Let stand at room temperature for 20 to 30 minutes. Fluff with a fork before serving. Store the leftovers in the refrigerator. **Yield:** 8 (1-cup) servings.

PER SERVING:
CALORIES: 58; CARBOHYDRATE: 9.4 g; PROTEIN: 2.2 g; TOTAL FAT: 1.9 g;
CHOLESTEROL: 0 mg; SODIUM: 57 mg; FIBER: 1 g;
CALORIES FROM FAT: 30%

FATTOUSH

Mint Dressing
4 garlic cloves ◆ ¹/₄ teaspoon salt
Juice of 3 lemons ◆ 1 tablespoon olive oil

Salad
1 (6-inch) pita round, split
8 cups thinly sliced romaine
1 cup chopped fresh tomatoes
¹/₂ cup shredded cabbage ◆ ¹/₂ cup thinly sliced green onions
¹/₂ cup chopped fresh parsley
1 small cucumber, chopped ◆ ¹/₄ cup chopped radishes
¹/₄ cup chopped bell pepper ◆ ¹/₈ teaspoon pepper
1 tablespoon dried mint, or 3 tablespoons chopped fresh mint
1 tablespoon ground sumac

For the dressing, mash the garlic and salt using a mortar and pestle until of a pasty consistency. Combine the garlic mixture, lemon juice and olive oil in a bowl and mix well.

For the salad, arrange the pita rounds in a single layer on a baking sheet. Spray lightly with olive oil-flavor nonstick cooking spray or garlic-flavor nonstick cooking spray. Toast at 400 degrees until light brown. Break the pita rounds into bite-size pieces. Toss the romaine, tomatoes, cabbage, green onions, parsley, cucumber, radishes, bell pepper and pepper in salad bowl. Add the dressing and toss to coat. Sprinkle with the mint and sumac and toss to mix. Add the pita pieces just before serving and mix well. Ground sumac is available in Middle Eastern markets.
Yield: 4 (2-cup) servings.

PER SERVING:
CALORIES: 127; CARBOHYDRATE: 20.2 g; PROTEIN: 5.1 g; TOTAL FAT: 4.5 g;
CHOLESTEROL: 0 mg; SODIUM: 248 mg; FIBER: 4.4 g;
CALORIES FROM FAT: 32%

CELEBRATIONS
AND SEASONS

Whole Wheat Pita Bread

1/2 teaspoon dry yeast
1 1/4 cups warm (105 to 115 degrees) water
1 1/4 cups whole wheat flour
1/2 teaspoon salt
1/2 teaspoon olive oil
1 3/4 cups bread flour

Dissolve the yeast in the warm water in a large bowl and mix well. Let stand for 5 minutes. Whisk 1 cup of the whole wheat flour into the yeast mixture until blended. Let rise, covered, in a warm place (85 degrees) free from drafts for 2 hours; the batter will be bubbly. Stir in the salt and olive oil. Stir in the bread flour with a wooden spoon. Knead the dough on a lightly floured surface for 10 minutes or until smooth and elastic, adding enough of the remaining 1/4 cup whole wheat flour 1 tablespoon at a time to prevent the dough from sticking to hands; the dough will feel tacky. Spray the inside of a large sealable plastic bag with nonstick cooking spray. Add the dough to the bag and seal tightly. Chill for 12 hours or overnight.

Place a pizza stone on the bottom oven rack. Preheat the oven to 500 degrees. Shape the dough into a 12-inch log on a lightly floured surface. Divide the log into 6 equal portions and cover to keep from drying out. Remove 1 portion at a time and shape into a ball. Let rest, covered, for 1 hour. Roll each ball into a 6-inch round on a lightly floured surface. Arrange 3 rounds on the pizza stone. Bake for 5 minutes. Place the pizza stone on the top oven rack. Bake for 2 minutes longer. Remove the rounds to a wire rack to cool. Repeat the baking process with the remaining 3 dough rounds. **Yield:** 6 servings.

PER SERVING:
CALORIES: 233; CARBOHYDRATE: 47.3 g; PROTEIN: 8.3 g; TOTAL FAT: 1.5 g; CHOLESTEROL: 0 mg; SODIUM: 195 mg; FIBER: 4.1 g; CALORIES FROM FAT: 6%

CELEBRATIONS
AND SEASONS

Baklava

1¼ cups ground or finely chopped walnuts
¾ cup wheat saltine cracker crumbs (about 20 crackers)
⅓ cup sugar ♦ ½ teaspoon cinnamon
12 sheets frozen phyllo pastry, thawed
1 cup sugar ♦ ½ cup water
¼ cup honey ♦ 2 teaspoons lemon juice

Combine the walnuts, cracker crumbs, ⅓ cup sugar and cinnamon in a bowl and mix well. Cover the pastry with a damp cotton towel or plastic wrap. Remove 1 pastry sheet and spray lightly with butter-flavor nonstick cooking spray. Fold the sheet crosswise into halves to form an 8×13-inch rectangle. Spray both sides lightly with butter-flavor nonstick cooking spray. Arrange the pastry rectangle in the bottom of a 9×13-inch baking dish sprayed with butter-flavor nonstick cooking spray. Sprinkle with 3 tablespoons of the walnut mixture. Repeat the process with 9 more sheets of the pastry and the remaining walnut mixture, spraying each layer lightly with butter-flavor nonstick cooking spray and ending with the walnut mixture.

Spray the remaining 2 sheets of pastry lightly with butter-flavor nonstick cooking spray. Fold each sheet crosswise into halves to form an 8×13-inch rectangle. Spray both sides lightly with butter-flavor nonstick cooking spray. Layer the 2 sheets over the prepared layers. Score the pastry ¾ inch deep in a diamond pattern with a sharp knife. Spray with butter-flavor nonstick cooking spray. Bake at 350 degrees for 30 minutes or until golden brown. Bring 1 cup sugar, water and honey to a boil in a saucepan, stirring occasionally. Stir in the lemon juice; reduce the heat. Simmer for 5 minutes, stirring frequently. Drizzle the sugar mixture over the baked layers. Cool in the pan on a wire rack. Cut into bars.
Yield: 18 (1-bar) servings.

Per Serving:
Calories: 186; Carbohydrate: 28.6 g; Protein: 2.2 g; Total Fat: 6.9 g;
Cholesterol: 0 mg; Sodium: 99 mg; Fiber: 1.3 g;
Calories from Fat: 33%

Follow these simple tips when using phyllo:

Always prepare the filling mixture first because phyllo dries out very quickly once it has been unwrapped and exposed to the air.

Remove only the number of thawed sheets called for at each step of the recipe, and place the sheets on a flat surface.

Keep the remaining phyllo sheets covered with a damp cotton towel or plastic wrap to prevent them from drying out.

Celebrations
and Seasons

Fruit and nuts are an important tradition in most Mediterranean countries. They are generally served after the main meal and before coffee and cake. Fruits include apples, bananas, oranges, and pears. Nuts include almonds, cashews, peanuts, pecans, and pistachios.

CELEBRATIONS
AND SEASONS

CHRISTMAS EVE TRADITION

White Wine
Baked Grouper with Chunky Tomato Sauce *page 27*
Savory Salmon Provençal *page 28*
Straight-From-Italy Tomato Sauce *page 64*
Assorted Fresh Fruit and Nuts
Pear Cake with Pine Nuts *page 29*
Espresso au Lait *page 75*

Baked Grouper with Chunky Tomato Sauce

3½ cups chopped seeded tomatoes (about 4 medium tomatoes)
¼ cup chopped green onions
¼ cup dry white wine
1 tablespoon chopped fresh basil
1 teaspoon capers
1 teaspoon minced garlic
1 teaspoon fresh lemon juice
⅛ teaspoon salt
¼ teaspoon crushed red pepper
¼ teaspoon black pepper
2 teaspoons olive oil
4 (6-inch) grouper fillets

Combine the tomatoes, green onions, wine, basil, capers, garlic, lemon juice, salt, red pepper and black pepper in a bowl and mix gently. Heat the olive oil in a large heavy ovenproof skillet over high heat. Arrange the fillets skin side up in the hot oil. Cook for 2 minutes; turn. Spoon the tomato mixture over the fillets. Bring to a boil. Bake at 425 degrees for 8 minutes or until the fillets flake easily when tested with a fork. **Yield:** 4 (1 fillet and ½ cup tomato sauce) servings.

PER SERVING:
CALORIES: 200; CARBOHYDRATE: 8.6 g; PROTEIN: 28 g; TOTAL FAT: 5.7 g;
CHOLESTEROL: 41 mg; SODIUM: 184 mg; FIBER: 2.2g;
CALORIES FROM FAT: 26%

CELEBRATIONS
AND SEASONS

SAVORY SALMON PROVENÇAL

1 red onion, thinly sliced and separated into rings
1 (1½-pound) salmon fillet
2 garlic cloves, minced
1 teaspoon herbes de Provence or dried Italian seasoning, crushed
¼ teaspoon pepper
1½ cups (1-inch-thick) slices plum tomatoes
1 (6-ounce) jar marinated artichoke hearts, drained
½ cup pitted kalamata olives, cut lengthwise into halves

Place the onion rings in a large foil baking bag. Arrange the fillet over the onion. Sprinkle with the garlic, ½ teaspoon of the herbes de Provence and pepper. Top with the tomatoes, artichokes and olives and sprinkle with the remaining ½ teaspoon herbes de Provence; seal the bag. Arrange the foil bag on a grill rack directly over medium-hot coals. Grill with the lid down for 20 to 25 minutes or until the fillet flakes easily when tested with a fork. Make a slit in the bag to allow the steam to escape. As an alternative to the foil bag, fold an 18×48-inch sheet of heavy-duty foil in half to make an 18×24-inch rectangle. Layer the fillet, seasonings, tomatoes, artichokes and olives in the center of the foil. Bring 2 sides of the foil together and seal with a double fold. Proceed as directed above. **Yield:** 6 servings.

PER SERVING:
CALORIES: 272; CARBOHYDRATE: 10 g; PROTEIN: 35 g; TOTAL FAT: 10 g;
CHOLESTEROL: 88 mg; SODIUM: 253 mg; FIBER: 2 g;
CALORIES FROM FAT: 33%

Pear Cake with Pine Nuts

1¹/₄ cups flour
³/₄ cup sugar
¹/₈ teaspoon salt
¹/₄ cup (¹/₂ stick) chilled margarine, cut into small pieces
2 tablespoons pine nuts, toasted
¹/₄ teaspoon cinnamon
¹/₃ cup fat-free sour cream
¹/₄ cup 1% milk
1 teaspoon grated lemon zest
1 teaspoon vanilla extract
¹/₂ teaspoon baking powder
¹/₄ teaspoon baking soda
1 egg
2 cups thinly sliced peeled pears

Spoon the flour lightly into a dry measuring cup and level with a knife. Combine the flour, sugar and salt in a bowl and stir with a whisk. Cut in the margarine with a pastry blender or 2 knives until crumbly. Mix ¹/₃ cup of the crumb mixture, pine nuts and cinnamon in a small bowl and set aside. Combine the remaining crumb mixture, sour cream, 1% milk, lemon zest, vanilla, baking powder, baking soda and egg in a mixing bowl. Beat at medium speed until blended. Spoon the batter into a 9-inch cake pan sprayed with nonstick cooking spray. Arrange the pear slices evenly over the batter and sprinkle with the pine nut mixture. Bake at 350 degrees for 45 minutes or until a wooden pick inserted in the center comes out clean. Cool in the pan on a wire rack. Always use margarine that has liquid oil listed as the first ingredient on the label.
Yield: 8 (1-wedge) servings.

Per Serving:
Calories: 252; Carbohydrate: 41.9 g; Protein: 4.2 g; Total Fat: 7.9 g;
Cholesterol: 26 mg; Sodium: 191; Fiber: 1.7g;
Calories from Fat: 28%

Celebrations
and Seasons

Holiday feasts are a family tradition in most Mediterranean countries. Since these holidays only occur a few times per year, families indulge in larger meals. These lavish meals include many courses of food. Extended members of the family and even close family friends attend these feasts. In Italy, twenty to thirty family members will attend such a feast. Courses are served one at a time and between courses there is festive conversation.

CELEBRATIONS
AND SEASONS

SPECIAL HOLIDAY FEAST

COURSE ONE: Soup
Lentil Soup *page 31*

COURSE TWO: Antipasto
Tomatoes with Mozzarella and Basil *page 86*
Roasted Peppers

COURSE THREE: Pasta
Eggplant Parmigiana *page 32*
Meat/Vegetable/Potato:
Pork Tenderloin with Pistachio Gremolata Crust *page 33*
Steamed Vegetables
Green Beans with Potatoes and Pesto *page 34*

COURSE FOUR: Fruit and Nuts
Mixed Marinated Fruit *page 35*
Assorted Fruit and Nuts
Cinnamon Rice Pudding with Dried Cherry Sauce *page 36*

COURSE FIVE: Coffee and Cake
Almond Biscotti *page 37*
Almond Cappuccino *page 75*

LENTIL SOUP

2 cups dried brown lentils
1 tablespoon olive oil
1 large onion, chopped
4 garlic cloves, minced
2 ribs celery, chopped
2 quarts water
1/2 teaspoon salt
Freshly ground pepper to taste
1 to 2 teaspoons cumin (optional)
Fresh lemon juice to taste
2 to 3 tablespoons chopped fresh parsley

Sort and rinse the lentils. Heat the olive oil in a heavy stockpot. Sauté the onion and garlic in the hot oil until the onion begins to color. Stir in the celery. Sauté for several minutes. Add the lentils and water and mix well. Bring to a boil; reduce the heat. Stir in the salt and pepper. Simmer, covered, for 30 to 40 minutes or until the lentils are tender, stirring occasionally. Stir in the cumin. Simmer for 5 to 10 minutes longer, stirring occasionally. Taste and adjust the seasonings. Ladle into soup bowls. Drizzle each serving with lemon juice and sprinkle with parsley. Serve immediately. For a smoother thicker soup, purée half or all the soup in a blender or food processor. Return the purée to the stockpot and cook just until heated through, stirring frequently. **Yield:** 6 (1¹/₂-cup) servings.

PER SERVING:
CALORIES: 129; CARBOHYDRATE: 28.8 g; PROTEIN: 11.2 g; TOTAL FAT: 2.4 g;
CHOLESTEROL: 0 mg; SODIUM: 211 mg; FIBER: 12 g;
CALORIES FROM FAT: 17%

CELEBRATIONS
AND SEASONS

Eggplant Parmigiana

3 cups egg substitute
3/4 cup grated reduced-fat Parmesan cheese or Romano cheese
1 1/2 teaspoons garlic powder, or 1 teaspoon crushed garlic
1 teaspoon basil
1 teaspoon onion powder
1/2 teaspoon pepper
3 medium firm eggplant, peeled and cut into 1-inch slices
3 cups Italian bread crumbs
5 cups Straight-From-Italy Tomato Sauce (page 64)
3 cups (12 ounces) shredded part-skim mozzarella cheese

Combine the egg substitute, 1/4 cup of the Parmesan cheese, garlic powder, basil, onion powder and pepper in a bowl and mix well. Dip the eggplant slices into the egg substitute mixture and coat with the bread crumbs. Arrange the slices in a single layer on a baking sheet sprayed with olive oil-flavor nonstick cooking spray. Bake at 350 degrees for 20 to 25 minutes or until tender. Dip the eggplant slices into the tomato sauce. Arrange half the eggplant slices in a large baking dish. Sprinkle with 1/4 cup of the Parmesan cheese and 1 cup of the mozzarella cheese. Layer with the remaining eggplant slices, remaining 1/4 cup Parmesan cheese and 1 cup of the mozzarella cheese. Bake, covered with foil, at 350 degrees for 20 minutes; remove the foil. Sprinkle with the remaining 1 cup mozzarella cheese. Bake until the cheese melts. Serve over hot cooked angel hair pasta. **Yield:** 12 servings.

Per Serving:
Calories: 257; Carbohydrate: 33.7 g; Protein: 10.6 g; Total Fat: 7 g;
Cholesterol: 4 mg; Sodium: 410 mg; Fiber: 4 g;
Calories from Fat: 25%

Celebrations
and Seasons

Pork Tenderloin with Pistachio Gremolata Crust

3/4 cup fresh parsley leaves
3 tablespoons pistachios
1 (1-ounce) slice hearty whole wheat bread, torn
1½ tablespoons finely grated lemon zest (1 to 2 lemons)
2 garlic cloves, minced
¼ teaspoon salt
1 tablespoon olive oil
1 (1-pound) pork tenderloin
1 egg white, lightly beaten
1 (15-ounce) can no-salt-added organic white beans
1 tablespoon red wine vinegar
1 tablespoon fat-free less-sodium chicken broth
Sprigs of parsley (optional)

Combine the parsley leaves, pistachios, bread, lemon zest, garlic and salt in a food processor. Process until crumbly. Add the olive oil. Pulse just until mixed. Trim the fat from the tenderloin. Dip the tenderloin in the egg white and coat with half the crumb mixture. Arrange the tenderloin on a nonstick baking sheet sprayed lightly with nonstick cooking spray. Bake at 375 degrees for 20 to 30 minutes or until a meat thermometer registers 160 degrees. Remove the tenderloin from the oven and cover with foil. Let rest for 5 minutes. Heat the beans in a saucepan or in a microwave-safe dish in the microwave. Add the remaining crumb mixture, vinegar and broth to the beans and mix well. Slice the pork and serve over the white bean mixture. Garnish with sprigs of parsley.
Yield: 4 (3 slices tenderloin and ½ cup beans) servings.

Per Serving:
Calories: 298; Carbohydrate: 19.4 g; Protein: 30.6 g; Total Fat: 13 g;
Cholesterol: 75 mg; Sodium: 208 mg; Fiber: 5.9 g;
Calories from Fat: 39%

Gremolata is a mixture of garlic, lemon, and fresh parsley. A little of the gremolata is also mixed into the white beans to offer a simple side dish to the pork.

Celebrations and Seasons

Pesto may be frozen for later use. Drop a tablespoon of pesto into each section of an ice tray and freeze. Remove frozen cubes and place in a heavy-duty sealable plastic bag. Let the pesto thaw for a few hours before you use it. Pesto will keep in the freezer for up to three months and in the refrigerator for up to five days.

CELEBRATIONS
AND SEASONS

GREEN BEANS WITH POTATOES AND PESTO

Pesto
2 cups loosely packed fresh basil leaves
1/3 cup (about 1 1/2 ounces) freshly grated Parmesan cheese
1/4 cup fat-free less-sodium chicken broth
2 garlic cloves, minced
1 tablespoon pine nuts
1 tablespoon olive oil
1/4 teaspoon salt
1/4 teaspoon freshly ground pepper

Vegetables
12 ounces fresh green beans, trimmed and cut into 1 1/2-inch pieces
1 1/4 pounds red potatoes, each cut into 6 wedges

For the pesto, combine the basil, cheese, broth, garlic, pine nuts, olive oil, salt and pepper in a food processor. Process until smooth.

For the vegetables, bring enough water to generously cover the green beans to a boil in a saucepan. Add the green beans. Cook until tender. Remove the beans with a slotted spoon to a bowl, reserving the liquid. Add the potatoes to the reserved liquid. Cook until the potatoes are tender; drain. Add the potatoes and pesto to the beans and toss to coat. **Yield:** 6 (1-cup) servings.

PER SERVING:
CALORIES: 148; CARBOHYDRATE: 20.8 g; PROTEIN: 6.5 g; TOTAL FAT: 5 g;
CHOLESTEROL: 5 mg; SODIUM: 243 mg; FIBER: 4.1 g;
CALORIES FROM FAT: 30%

Mixed Marinated Fruit

(Macedonia di Frutta)

2 cups chopped cantaloupe
2 kiwifruit, peeled, cut into halves lengthwise and thinly sliced
1 cup chopped peeled peach
1 cup chopped strawberries
1 cup blueberries
2/3 cup chopped peeled nectarine
1/2 cup fresh orange juice (about 1 orange)
1/4 cup sugar
2 tablespoons grappa (Italian brandy) or brandy (optional)
1 1/2 teaspoons grated lemon zest

Toss the cantaloupe, kiwifruit, peach, strawberries, blueberries and nectarine in a bowl. Add the orange juice, sugar, brandy and lemon zest and mix gently until coated. Chill, covered, for 2 hours.
Yield: 5 (1-cup) servings.

Per Serving:
Calories: 154; Carbohydrate: 34.8 g; Protein: 1.8 g; Total Fat: 0.7 g;
Cholesterol: 0 mg; Sodium: 10 mg; Fiber: 4.2 g;
Calories from Fat: 4%

Celebrations
and Seasons

Cinnamon Rice Pudding with Dried Cherry Sauce

Cinnamon Rice Pudding

6 cups water ◆ 1 1/2 cups jasmine rice
1 (3-inch) cinnamon stick
1/4 teaspoon salt ◆ 3 cups 1% milk ◆ 1/2 cup sugar
1 teaspoon ground cinnamon
1 teaspoon vanilla extract ◆ 1/2 teaspoon almond extract

Dried Cherry Sauce

1 1/2 cups water ◆ 1 cup dried tart cherries
2 tablespoons sugar ◆ 1 tablespoon water
1 teaspoon cornstarch ◆ 1/2 teaspoon vanilla extract
1/4 teaspoon almond extract

For the pudding, combine the water, rice, cinnamon stick and salt in a large heavy saucepan. Bring to a boil; reduce the heat. Simmer for 20 minutes or until the rice is tender, stirring occasionally; drain. Add the 1% milk, sugar and ground cinnamon to the rice mixture and mix well. Bring to a simmer over medium heat, stirring occasionally. Reduce the heat to medium-low. Cook for 30 minutes or until thickened, stirring frequently. Discard the cinnamon stick. Remove from the heat. Stir in the flavorings. Cover to keep warm.

For the sauce, combine 1 1/2 cups water and the cherries in a medium saucepan. Bring to a boil; reduce the heat. Simmer for 20 minutes, stirring occasionally. Stir in the sugar. Cook for 5 minutes, stirring occasionally. Mix 1 tablespoon water and the cornstarch in a small bowl. Stir the cornstarch mixture into the cherry mixture. Bring to a boil. Boil for 1 minute or until slightly thickened, stirring constantly. Remove from the heat. Stir in the flavorings. Serve with the warm pudding. **Yield:** 8 (3/4 cup pudding and 2 1/2 tablespoons sauce) servings.

Per Serving:
Calories: 283; Carbohydrate: 61.4 g; Protein: 6.2 g; Total Fat: 1.3 g;
Cholesterol: 7 mg; Sodium: 106 mg; Fiber: 1.2 g;
Calories from Fat: 4%

Almond Biscotti

2 cups flour
1 cup sugar
1/3 cup slivered almonds, toasted and chopped
3/4 teaspoon baking soda
1/8 teaspoon salt
2 eggs, lightly beaten
1 egg white, lightly beaten
1 teaspoon vanilla extract
1/4 teaspoon almond extract

Combine the flour, sugar, almonds, baking soda and salt in a bowl and mix well. Whisk the eggs, egg white and flavorings in a bowl until blended. Add the egg mixture to the flour mixture and stir until blended; the dough will be dry. Knead the dough lightly on a lightly floured surface 7 times. Shape into a 16-inch-long log. Arrange the log on a baking sheet sprayed with nonstick cooking spray; flatten to 1 inch thick.

Bake at 350 degrees for 30 minutes. Cool the log on a wire rack for 10 minutes. Cut the log diagonally into thirty 1/2-inch slices. Arrange the slices cut side down on the baking sheet. Reduce the oven temperature to 325 degrees. Bake for 10 minutes; turn. Bake for 10 minutes longer. Remove the slices to a wire rack to cool; the slices will be slightly soft in the center but will harden as they cool. **Yield:** 30 (1-slice) servings.

Per Serving:
Calories: 66; Carbohydrate: 12.9 g; Protein: 1.5 g; Total Fat: 1g;
Cholesterol: 14 mg; Sodium: 37 mg; Fiber: 0.5 g;
Calories from Fat: 14%

Celebrations
and Seasons

Simply Mediterranean

Most of us live fast-paced lives. We often find that we are eating lunch in our cars or at our desks—or skipping it altogether—in an effort to save time. By contrast, one key ingredient to the healthy Mediterranean diet is time.

Lunch is the most elaborate meal of the day, and it can take one and one-half hours, with a nap or siesta afterward. Sounds wonderful, doesn't it? And it's healthy. Placing your largest meal in the middle of the day helps with digestion and helps you sleep better at night. It also gives you time to burn off excess calories.

So if we do not have time to eat right, how can we find the time to cook right? It can be done! Take heart—and take a look at the following thirty-minutes-or-less recipes.

Eating Mediterranean style
entails more than using
olive oil in food preparation:

Eat together as a family.

Use olive oil instead
of other fats.

Get rid of the butter.

Cut down on meat portions.

Choose water as the
beverage of choice.

Limit alcohol to a glass of
wine with meals.

Increase the amount and
variety of vegetables eaten.

Include a crisp green salad
at both lunch and dinner.
Choose dark leafy greens
instead of iceberg.

Search for a good source for
dense, chewy, whole grain
loaves of bread.

Add other fiber-rich sources
of whole grains such as
brown rice, whole wheat
pasta, and bulgur.

SIMPLY MEDITERRANEAN

MEDITERRANEAN CHICKEN PASTA

16 ounces penne
1 pound chicken tenders, cut into 1-inch pieces
1 red onion, vertically sliced
4 garlic cloves, minced
1 cup artichoke hearts, cut into quarters
2/3 cup pesto
1/2 cup black olives, sliced
2 Roma tomatoes, coarsely chopped
3 ounces feta cheese, crumbled
1/2 cup white wine

Cook the pasta using package directions, omitting the fat and salt; drain. Cover to keep warm. Sauté the chicken in a large nonstick skillet sprayed with olive oil-flavor nonstick cooking spray until the chicken is no longer pink. Stir in the onion and garlic. Sauté until the onion is tender. Add the artichokes, pesto and olives. Simmer for 6 minutes or until heated through, stirring occasionally. Add the pasta, tomatoes, cheese and wine and mix well. Cook just until heated through, stirring frequently. Serve immediately. **Yield:** 8 servings.

PER SERVING:
CALORIES: 384; CARBOHYDRATE: 48.7 g; PROTEIN: 28.7 g; TOTAL FAT: 10.3 g;
CHOLESTEROL: 59.7 mg; SODIUM: 379 mg; FIBER: 3.7 g;
CALORIES FROM FAT: 24%

PASTA WITH GARBANZO BEANS

2 teaspoons olive oil ♦ 2 cups chopped tomatoes
2 garlic cloves, minced
3 cups hot cooked angel hair pasta (about 6 ounces uncooked)
1 (15-ounce) can garbanzo beans or chick-peas, drained
1/2 cup chopped fresh basil ♦ 1/8 teaspoon salt ♦ 1/4 teaspoon pepper
1/2 cup (2 ounces) grated asiago cheese or Parmesan cheese
2 tablespoons balsamic vinegar ♦ Sprigs of basil (optional)

Heat the olive oil in a large nonstick skillet over medium-high heat. Sauté the tomatoes and garlic in the hot oil for 2 minutes. Stir in the pasta, beans, chopped basil, salt and pepper. Cook for 2 minutes. Mix the pasta mixture, cheese and vinegar in a serving bowl. Garnish with sprigs of basil. **Yield:** 4 (1¼-cup) servings.

PER SERVING:
CALORIES: 376; CARBOHYDRATE: 57.8 g; PROTEIN: 17.5 g; TOTAL FAT: 8.9 g;
CHOLESTEROL: 15 mg; SODIUM:408 mg; FIBER: 4.9 g;
CALORIES FROM FAT: 21%

PASTA WITH WATERCRESS, TOMATOES AND GOAT CHEESE

12 ounces tubetti (short tubular pasta) ♦ 4 cups cherry tomato halves
4 cups chopped trimmed watercress (about 8 ounces)
1 cup (4 ounces) crumbled goat cheese ♦ 2 garlic cloves, minced
1/2 teaspoon pepper ♦ 1/4 teaspoon salt

Cook the pasta using package directions, omitting the fat and salt. Toss with the remaining ingredients in a bowl. **Yield:** 6 (2-cup) servings.

PER SERVING:
CALORIES: 285; CARBOHYDRATE: 47.5 g; PROTEIN: 12.1 g; TOTAL FAT: 5.2 g;
CHOLESTEROL: 9 mg; SODIUM: 190 mg; FIBER: 3.3 g;
CALORIES FROM FAT: 16%

SIMPLY
MEDITERRANEAN

Fresh Vegetables and Linguini

4 ounces linguini
1 teaspoon olive oil
1/4 cup chopped onion
1 (4-ounce) zucchini, sliced
1 garlic clove, minced
1 tomato, peeled and cut into 8 wedges
1/2 cup low-fat less-sodium chicken broth
1/4 cup sliced mushrooms
2 tablespoons white wine
1/4 teaspoon Italian seasoning
1/8 teaspoon salt
Freshly ground pepper
1 tablespoon grated Parmesan cheese made with skim milk

Cook the pasta using package directions, omitting the fat and salt; drain. Cover to keep warm. Heat the olive oil in a medium nonstick skillet. Sauté the onion, zucchini and garlic in the hot oil until the vegetables are tender-crisp. Stir in the tomato, broth, mushrooms, wine, Italian seasoning and salt. Bring to a boil; reduce the heat to medium-low. Cook for 3 to 4 minutes, stirring frequently. Place the pasta in a serving bowl. Add the zucchini mixture and pepper and toss to mix. Sprinkle with the cheese. **Yield:** 2 servings.

Per Serving:
Calories: 277; Carbohydrate: 50 g; Protein: 10 g; Total Fat: 5 g;
Cholesterol: 3 mg; Sodium: 195 mg; Fiber: 2 g;
Calories from Fat: 16%

Simply
Mediterranean

Tomato and Pesto Pizza

Basil Pesto
4 cups fresh basil leaves
2 garlic cloves
1/4 cup fat-free less-sodium chicken broth
1 tablespoon freshly grated Parmesan cheese
1 tablespoon olive oil

Pizza
1 (1-pound) Italian cheese-flavor pizza crust, such as Boboli
3 cups chopped seeded tomatoes (about 2 pounds)
3 garlic cloves, thinly sliced
1 cup (4 ounces) shredded part-skim mozzarella cheese
1/4 cup julienned fresh basil leaves

For the pesto, combine the basil and garlic in a food processor. Pulse 5 times or until coarsely chopped. Add the broth, cheese and olive oil, processing constantly until blended.

For the pizza, arrange the pizza crust on a baking sheet. Spread the pesto over the crust to within 1/2 inch of the edge. Top with the tomatoes, garlic and cheese. Bake at 475 degrees for 8 to 10 minutes or until the cheese melts. Sprinkle with the basil. Cut into 8 wedges.
Yield: 8 (1-wedge) servings.

PER SERVING:
CALORIES: 228; CARBOHYDRATE: 29.1 g; PROTEIN: 11 g; TOTAL FAT: 7.5 g;
CHOLESTEROL: 10 mg; SODIUM: 400 mg; FIBER: 1.7 g;
CALORIES FROM FAT: 30%

Foods vary from country to country, but in general the Mediterranean diet consists of eight guidelines:

High in monounsaturated fats and low in saturated and trans fats

High in beans and lentils

High in grain foods (such as bread, pasta, couscous, and rice)

High in fruits

High in vegetables and herbs

Low in meat and meat products, especially red meat

Moderate in milk and dairy products (mostly yogurt and cheese)

Moderate in alcohol (usually wine and always with food)

Simply Mediterranean

ROASTED VEGETABLE PIZZA

1 (10-ounce) can refrigerated pizza crust dough
1 small onion, cut into 12 wedges
1 small yellow squash, cut into 1/4-inch slices
1 small red bell pepper, cut into 2-inch pieces
4 garlic cloves, thinly sliced
2 tablespoons balsamic vinegar
1 tablespoon chopped fresh thyme, or 1 teaspoon dried thyme
1 teaspoon olive oil
1/8 teaspoon salt
1 1/4 cups (5 ounces) shredded sharp provolone cheese

Unroll the pizza dough onto a large baking sheet sprayed with nonstick cooking spray. Fold under the edges of the dough to form an 11-inch circle. Bake at 425 degrees for 7 minutes. Increase the oven temperature to 500 degrees. Combine the onion, squash, bell pepper, garlic, vinegar, thyme, olive oil and salt in a bowl and toss to mix. Spread the vegetable mixture in a 9×13-inch baking dish. Roast for 15 minutes, stirring halfway through the roasting process. Reduce the oven temperature to 425 degrees. Sprinkle half the cheese over the pizza crust. Top with the roasted vegetables and sprinkle with the remaining cheese. Bake for 12 minutes or until the crust is light brown. **Yield:** 6 (1-slice) servings.

PER SERVING:
CALORIES: 293; CARBOHYDRATE: 40.2 g; PROTEIN: 10 g; TOTAL FAT: 8.8 g;
CHOLESTEROL: 16 mg; SODIUM: 491 mg; FIBER: 2.8 g;
CALORIES FROM FAT: 27%

Polenta with Herbed Vinaigrette

1 (16-ounce) tube refrigerated polenta
1 1/2 teaspoons olive oil
2 tablespoons balsamic vinegar
1 teaspoon minced fresh basil
1 teaspoon minced fresh oregano
1 teaspoon minced fresh parsley
1 teaspoon minced garlic
Pepper to taste
1 tablespoon shredded Parmesan cheese

Cut the polenta into 6 equal slices. Heat the olive oil in a large nonstick skillet. Sear the polenta in the hot oil until brown on both sides. Remove the polenta to an ovenproof dish. Keep warm in a 250-degree oven; do not hold longer than 20 minutes. Combine the vinegar, basil, oregano, parsley, garlic and pepper in the same skillet used to sear the polenta and mix well. Cook until slightly reduced, stirring frequently. Pour the vinaigrette over the warm polenta. Sprinkle with the cheese. Serve immediately. **Yield:** 6 (2 1/2-ounce) servings.

Per Serving:
Calories: 88; Carbohydrate: 15.7 g; Protein: 2.4 g; Total Fat: 1.4 g;
Cholesterol: 0.6 mg; Sodium: 325 mg; Fiber: 1 g;
Calories from Fat: 14%

Simply
Mediterranean

MEDITERRANEAN MAKEOVERS

The Mediterranean diet includes a wide variety of grains, beans, fresh fruits and vegetables, seafood, poultry, cheese, eggs, and small portions of lean meat. They are all good foods, and more importantly, they are prepared in a way that preserves their health benefits.

That's where this region excels. For example, many Mediterranean recipes are prepared in olive oil. Naturally cholesterol-free, olive oil has been shown to produce less harmful and more beneficial effects than other vegetable oils.

Let's look at some delicious recipes that have been modified slightly to be even better for us. You might say we've taken not-so-healthy recipes and given them a Mediterranean Makeover.

Seven-Layer Italian Salad

Dijon Vinaigrette
1/4 cup red wine vinegar
1/4 cup water
1 tablespoon extra-virgin olive oil
2 teaspoons Dijon mustard
1 teaspoon Italian seasoning
1 teaspoon minced fresh garlic
1/2 teaspoon pepper
1/4 teaspoon Tabasco sauce

Salad
3 cups thinly sliced romaine
1 medium red bell pepper, julienned
1 medium cucumber, sliced
2 cups yellow or red teardrop tomatoes, cut into halves
1 medium yellow bell pepper, cut into 1/2-inch pieces
1 cup thinly sliced celery
3/4 cup sliced green onions
1/2 cup (2 ounces) shredded nonfat mozzarella cheese
Red bell pepper rings (optional)

For the vinaigrette, whisk the vinegar, water, olive oil, Dijon mustard, Italian seasoning, garlic, pepper and Tabasco sauce in a small bowl until mixed.

For the salad, layer the romaine, 1 julienned red bell pepper, cucumber, tomatoes, yellow bell pepper, celery and green onions in the order listed in a 3-quart salad bowl. Drizzle with the vinaigrette; do not toss. Sprinkle with the cheese. Chill, covered, until serving time. Garnish with red bell pepper rings. **Yield:** 8 servings.

PER SERVING:
CALORIES: 61; CARBOHYDRATE: 7.6 g; PROTEIN: 3.8 g; TOTAL FAT: 2.3 g;
CHOLESTEROL: 1 mg; SODIUM: 115 mg; FIBER: 1.7 g;
CALORIES FROM FAT: 34%

Herbed Fish and Vegetable Packets

4 (4- to 6-ounce) frozen cod, sole or haddock fillets, thawed
1/2 teaspoon thyme
1/2 teaspoon marjoram
4 teaspoons lemon juice
1 (16-ounce) package frozen broccoli, carrots and cauliflower
1/4 cup chopped green onions
Pepper to taste
4 teaspoons olive oil

Cut four 12×18-inch sheets of heavy-duty foil and spray 1 side with butter-flavor nonstick cooking spray. Place 1 fillet in the center of each sheet of foil. Sprinkle with the thyme and marjoram and drizzle with the lemon juice. Arrange 1/4 of the frozen vegetables around each fillet and sprinkle with the green onions and pepper. Drizzle with the olive oil. Bring the 2 long sides of the foil together and double fold the top and ends to seal, leaving room for heat circulation inside the packet. Place the packets on a baking sheet. Bake at 450 degrees for 18 to 22 minutes or until the fillets flake easily. Or you may place the packets on a grill rack over hot coals. Grill with the lid down for 16 to 20 minutes or until the fillets flake easily. **Yield:** 4 servings.

Per Serving:
Calories: 256; Carbohydrate: 9 g; Protein: 42 g; Total Fat: 6 g;
Cholesterol: 63 mg; Sodium: 220 mg; Fiber: 1.9 g;
Calories from Fat: 21%

Try this Tomato Tarragon Topping over baked or grilled halibut or cod fillets. Sauté 1/2 cup finely chopped onion and 1/4 cup finely chopped celery in 1 teaspoon olive oil in a skillet for 1 minute. Stir in 1 1/2 cups seeded chopped plum tomatoes. Sauté for 1 1/2 minutes or until the tomatoes are tender. Remove from the heat. Stir in 1 tablespoon lemon juice, 1 1/2 teaspoons chopped fresh tarragon, 1/4 teaspoon salt and 1/8 teaspoon pepper. Spoon over the fillets.

Mediterranean Makeovers

Spinach- and Feta-Stuffed Shells with Tomato Sauce

Spinach and Feta Filling

1 (10-ounce) package frozen chopped spinach, thawed and drained
1/2 cup (2 ounces) crumbled feta cheese
1/2 cup fat-free ricotta cheese ♦ 1 tablespoon chopped walnuts, toasted
1 egg white, lightly beaten ♦ 1/4 teaspoon cinnamon
1/4 teaspoon pepper

Tomato Sauce and Assembly

1 (14-ounce) can diced no-salt-added tomatoes
1/2 (6-ounce) can no-salt-added tomato paste (1/3 cup)
2 tablespoons water ♦ 1 teaspoon sugar
1/4 teaspoon garlic powder ♦ 12 jumbo pasta shells
1 tablespoon chopped walnuts, toasted
1/4 cup (1 ounce) fat-free shredded mozzarella cheese

For the filling, press the excess moisture from the spinach. Combine the spinach, feta cheese, ricotta cheese, walnuts, egg white, cinnamon and pepper in a bowl and mix well.

For the sauce, combine the undrained tomatoes, tomato paste, water, sugar and garlic powder in a medium saucepan and mix well. Bring to a boil; reduce the heat. Simmer for 5 minutes or until slightly thickened, stirring occasionally.

To serve, stuff each shell with approximately 2 tablespoons of the filling. Arrange the shells in a single layer in an ungreased 2-quart baking dish. Spoon the sauce over the shells and sprinkle with the walnuts. Bake, covered, at 350 degrees for 25 minutes. Sprinkle with the cheese. Bake for 2 to 3 minutes longer or until the cheese melts. **Yield**: 4 servings.

Per Serving:
Calories: 386; Carbohydrate: 58.3 g; Protein: 22 g; Total Fat: 6.4 g;
Cholesterol: 26.5 mg; Sodium: 312 mg; Fiber: 3.9 g;
Calories from Fat: 15%

Stuffed Bell Peppers

2 cups no-salt-added tomato juice ◆ 4 large green bell peppers
1 tablespoon olive oil ◆ 4 tomatoes, chopped
2 onions, sliced ◆ 1 medium zucchini, chopped
2 garlic cloves, minced ◆ 2 cups cooked brown rice
½ cup (2 ounces) shredded low-fat Cheddar cheese

Pour the tomato juice into a shallow baking dish. Cut the tops from the bell peppers, reserving the tops. Discard the seeds and membranes. Heat the olive oil in a nonstick skillet sprayed with nonstick cooking spray over medium heat. Sauté the tomatoes, onions, zucchini and garlic in the hot oil until the zucchini is tender-crisp. Mix the brown rice and cheese in a bowl. Add the rice mixture to the zucchini mixture and mix well. Spoon the rice mixture into the bell pepper shells and top with the reserved tops. Arrange the bell peppers upright in the prepared baking dish. Bake at 375 degrees for 30 minutes. **Yield:** 4 servings.

PER SERVING:
CALORIES: 264; CARBOHYDRATE: 46 g; PROTEIN: 10 g; TOTAL FAT: 6.2 g;
CHOLESTEROL: 3 mg; SODIUM: 120 mg; FIBER: 6.2 g;
CALORIES FROM FAT: 21%

Sautéed Green Beans with Garlic

¾ cup water ◆ 1 pound fresh green beans, trimmed
3 garlic cloves, minced ◆ ⅛ teaspoon salt ◆ ⅛ teaspoon pepper

Bring the water to a boil in a large nonstick skillet. Add the beans. Cook for 3 minutes; drain. Heat a large nonstick skillet sprayed with nonstick cooking spray over medium-high heat. Sauté the beans and garlic in the hot skillet for 1 minute. Sprinkle the beans with the salt and pepper. Sauté for 1 minute longer. **Yield:** 4 (1-cup) servings.

PER SERVING:
CALORIES: 50; CARBOHYDRATE: 9.9 g; PROTEIN: 2.3 g; TOTAL FAT: TRACE;
CHOLESTEROL: 0 mg; SODIUM: 78 mg; FIBER: 2.4 g;
CALORIES FROM FAT: 0%

Help control your weight by using these tips:

Eat slowly like Europeans in Mediterranean countries.

Eat less fat and more complex carbohydrates like whole grains, fruits, and vegetables. In Egypt, the diet is very heavy on legumes such as fava beans and lentils.

Limit your intake of butter, ice cream, cheese, salad dressings, and oil. In many Mediterranean countries people do eat these types of foods, but in small quantities.

Exercise regularly. Staying physically active increases the total number of calories you burn each day.

MEDITERRANEAN
MAKEOVERS

MEDITERRANEAN
MAKEOVERS

LEMONY HERBED ASPARAGUS

1 pound fresh asparagus spears ◆ 1¹/2 teaspoons olive oil
¹/8 teaspoon basil, crushed ◆ ¹/8 teaspoon oregano, crushed
¹/8 teaspoon pepper ◆ 1 teaspoon lemon juice

Snap off the woody ends of the asparagus spears and remove the scales. Place a vegetable steamer basket in a saucepan. Add water to just below the basket and bring to a boil. Place the asparagus in the basket. Steam, covered, for 5 to 8 minutes or until tender-crisp. Mix the olive oil, basil, oregano and pepper in a small saucepan. Cook over medium heat until heated through, stirring constantly. Remove from the heat. Stir in the lemon juice. Arrange the asparagus on a serving platter and spray with butter-flavor nonstick cooking spray. Drizzle with the lemon mixture. **Yield:** 4 servings.

PER SERVING:
CALORIES:58; CARBOHYDRATE: 5 g; PROTEIN: 3 g; TOTAL FAT: 1.9 g;
CHOLESTEROL: 0 mg; SODIUM: 5 mg; FIBER: 1.4 g;
CALORIES FROM FAT: 29%

"MEDITERRANEAN" GREENS

1 teaspoon olive oil ◆ 1 small onion, sliced
2 (10-ounce) packages frozen turnip greens or mixed greens
1 teaspoon low-sodium beef bouillon ◆ ¹/8 teaspoon salt
1 to 2 cups water

Spray a saucepan with nonstick cooking spray. Add the olive oil and onion to the prepared saucepan. Sauté until the onion is tender. Add the turnip greens, bouillon and salt and just enough of the water to cover. Cook, covered, for 1 hour or until the greens are tender, adding additional water as needed. **Yield:** 6 (¹/2-cup) servings.

PER SERVING:
CALORIES:33; CARBOHYDRATE: 4.6 g; PROTEIN: 2.4 g; TOTAL FAT: 1 g;
CHOLESTEROL: 0 mg; SODIUM: 58 mg; FIBER: 2.6 g;
CALORIES FROM FAT: 27%

Streusel Fig Muffins

Streusel Topping
¹/₃ cup packed brown sugar
¹/₄ cup quick-cooking oats
2 tablespoons finely chopped walnuts
1 teaspoon vanilla extract ♦ Pump-spray margarine

Fig Muffins
1¹/₄ cups whole wheat flour
1¹/₄ cups all-purpose flour
¹/₂ cup sugar
1 teaspoon baking powder
1 teaspoon baking soda
¹/₂ teaspoon salt ♦ 1 cup buttermilk
3 tablespoons olive oil
1 egg, lightly beaten
2 teaspoons vanilla extract
1¹/₂ cups chopped fresh figs

For the topping, combine the brown sugar, oats, walnuts and vanilla in a bowl and mix until crumbly, adding spray margarine as needed for the desired consistency.

For the muffins, combine the whole wheat flour, all-purpose flour, sugar, baking powder, baking soda and salt in a bowl and mix well. Make a well in the center of the flour mixture. Whisk the buttermilk, olive oil, egg and vanilla in a bowl until blended. Stir in the figs. Add the fig mixture to the well and stir just until moistened. Spoon the batter into 18 muffin cups sprayed with nonstick cooking spray. Sprinkle with the topping. Bake at 400 degrees for 18 to 20 minutes or until a wooden pick inserted in the center of the muffins comes out clean. Remove the muffins immediately to a wire rack to cool. **Yield:** 18 (1-muffin) servings.

Per Serving:
Calories: 151; Carbohydrate: 26.3 g; Protein: 3.1 g; Total Fat: 3.8 g;
Cholesterol: 12 mg; Sodium: 150 mg; Fiber: 1.8 g;
Calories from Fat: 23%

Mediterranean Makeovers

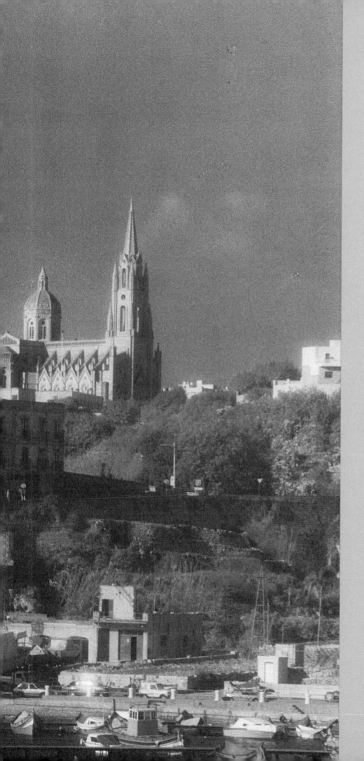

TRADITIONS IN THE MAKING

We all have traditions, and many center around food. Who has not treasured a family recipe passed down to us by our mother or grandmother?

Traditions are just as important in the Mediterranean. In Morocco, for example, diffas, or feasts, are held on special occasions, including anniversaries of saints, birthdays, and weddings. Weddings are by far the most elaborate and festive of all the events in the Moroccan culture.

Guests are welcomed with a glass of mint tea and a tray full of plump dates and dried almonds. The bride is dressed elaborately and seated in a large wooden chair that resembles a throne.

A traditional hand-washing ceremony kicks off the feast. Guests hold their hands above a copper basin while a servant pours warm water over them. Then the guests are given a few drops of orange flower water to rub into the palms of their hands. Once the hands are clean, the food is served.

Your are invited to try these recipes from the Mediterranean and discover what makes them treasures.

MOUSSAKA

3 medium potatoes, peeled and cut into 1/4-inch slices
2 small eggplant, peeled and cut into 1/2-inch slices
1 1/2 pounds extra-lean ground beef or ground lamb
2 cups chopped onions ♦ 1 (8-ounce) can tomato sauce
1/2 cup dry red wine or water ♦ 3 garlic cloves, minced
1 tablespoon minced fresh oregano, or 1 teaspoon dried oregano
Pepper to taste ♦ 2 1/4 teaspoons extra-virgin olive oil
1/4 cup flour ♦ 2 cups 1% milk
1/2 cup freshly grated Parmesan cheese

Arrange the potatoes in a single layer on a baking sheet sprayed with nonstick cooking spray. Spray the potatoes with nonstick cooking spray. Broil until brown on both sides; the potatoes do not need to be cooked through. Spray both sides of the eggplant slices with nonstick cooking spray and arrange in a single layer on a baking sheet. Broil for 5 minutes. Turn the slices and spray with nonstick cooking spray. Broil until brown. Brown the ground beef with the onions in a large skillet until the ground beef is crumbly; drain. Stir in the tomato sauce, wine, garlic, oregano and pepper. Simmer for 10 minutes, stirring occasionally.

Heat the olive oil in a saucepan over medium heat. Stir in the flour. Cook until bubbly, stirring constantly. Add the 1% milk gradually, stirring constantly. Bring to a gentle boil. Cook until thickened and of a sauce consistency, stirring constantly. Remove from the heat. Add the cheese and stir until blended. Layer 1/2 of the eggplant, 1/2 of the potatoes and 1/2 of the ground beef mixture in a 9×13-inch baking pan sprayed with nonstick cooking spray. Top with the remaining potatoes, remaining eggplant and remaining ground beef mixture. Spoon the cheese sauce over the top. Bake at 350 degrees for 45 to 60 minutes or until golden brown. Let stand for 15 to 20 minutes before serving. **Yield:** 8 servings.

PER SERVING:
CALORIES: 271; CARBOHYDRATE: 21.4 g; PROTEIN: 22.5 g; TOTAL FAT: 10.2 g;
CHOLESTEROL: 52 mg; SODIUM: 322 mg; FIBER: 2.9 g;
CALORIES FROM FAT: 34%

Lamb Shanks with Cannellini Beans

Cannellini Beans
1 cup dried cannellini beans or other white beans
2 teaspoons olive oil ◆ 4 garlic cloves, sliced

Lamb and Assembly
6 (12-ounce) lamb shanks, trimmed ◆ 1/4 teaspoon each salt and pepper
2 cups minced carrots ◆ 1 cup minced onion ◆ 1 cup minced celery
1 cup dry red wine ◆ 2 (14-ounce) cans diced no-salt-added tomatoes
1/2 cup fat-free beef broth ◆ 1 1/2 teaspoons rosemary ◆ 2 bay leaves

For the beans, sort and rinse the beans. Combine the beans with enough water to measure 2 inches above the beans in a Dutch oven. Boil for 2 minutes. Remove from the heat. Let stand, covered, for 1 hour; drain. Combine the beans with enough water to measure 2 inches above the beans. Bring to a boil; reduce the heat. Simmer for 1 hour or until tender. Drain the beans and place in a bowl. Heat the olive oil in the Dutch oven over medium-high heat. Sauté the garlic in the hot oil for 2 minutes or until golden brown. Stir in the beans. Remove from the heat and cover.

For the lamb, sprinkle the lamb with the salt and pepper. Brown the lamb on all sides in a nonstick skillet over medium-high heat for 12 minutes. Remove the lamb to a platter, reserving the pan drippings. Sauté the carrots, onion and celery in the reserved pan drippings for 3 minutes. Stir in the wine. Bring to a boil. Boil for 5 minutes, stirring frequently. Stir in the undrained tomatoes, broth, rosemary and bay leaves. Return the lamb to the skillet. Simmer, covered, for 2 hours or until the lamb is very tender, turning once. Remove the lamb to a platter with a slotted spoon, reserving the pan liquids and cover to keep warm. Bring the reserved pan liquids to a boil. Boil for 5 minutes or until slightly thickened, stirring occasionally. Discard the bay leaves.

To serve, divide the beans evenly among 6 serving plates. Top each serving with 1 lamb shank and drizzle with the sauce. **Yield:** 6 (1 lamb shank, 2/3 cup beans and 1 1/3 cups sauce) servings.

PER SERVING:
CALORIES: 496; CARBOHYDRATE: 32.9 g; PROTEIN: 60.2 g; TOTAL FAT: 13.9 g;
CHOLESTEROL: 156 mg; SODIUM: 255 mg; FIBER: 6.3 g;
CALORIES FROM FAT: 25%

Store cooked beans in airtight containers for up to five days in the refrigerator or six months in the freezer.

Dried beans have a shelf life of six months to a year. Store in airtight glass jars, away from heat.

1 cup dried beans = 2 to 2 1/2 cups of cooked beans.

Bean: water ratio is 1 cup of dried beans to 4 cups of water.

Beans are fully cooked when you can mash them with a fork.

Dried beans should be smooth and bright.

Old beans may be dull, wrinkled, or have cracked seams.

Traditions in the Making

Meloukhia, a leafy green, is traditionally the main ingredient of this recipe. Because it is hard to find, spinach, turnip greens, and/or mustard greens are often used as an alternative.

TRADITIONS IN THE MAKING

MIDDLE EASTERN GREENS WITH CHICKEN
(MELOUKHIA)

1 (2½-pound) chicken, skinned
8 cups water ◆ 1 large onion, cut into halves
1 cinnamon stick
20 ounces or 2 large bunches fresh spinach, turnip greens or
mustard greens
1 tablespoon olive oil ◆ ⅓ cup fresh cilantro, chopped
10 garlic cloves, crushed ◆ ¼ teaspoon salt
½ teaspoon pepper ◆ 2 cups hot cooked rice
½ cup red wine vinegar ◆ ½ cup chopped onion
½ cup crumbled toasted pita bread

Combine the chicken, water, 1 large onion and cinnamon stick in an 8-quart Dutch oven or stockpot. Bring to a boil; reduce the heat to medium. Cook for 1 hour. Remove the chicken to a bowl, reserving the broth. Strain the reserved broth into a bowl through a colander lined with cheesecloth or a fine sieve. Reserve the onion and discard the remaining solids. Return the broth to the Dutch oven. Chop the chicken into bite-size pieces, discarding the bones. Cover the chicken to keep warm. Mash the reserved onion in a bowl with a fork or potato masher. Add the onion to the broth. Bring to a boil. Add the spinach in batches to the broth mixture. Cook until the spinach wilts.

Heat the olive oil in a small nonstick skillet over medium-high heat. Sauté the cilantro, garlic and salt in the hot oil for 30 seconds or until the garlic begins to brown. Add the garlic mixture to the spinach mixture and mix well. Stir in the pepper. Cook until the spinach is tender, stirring occasionally. To serve, spoon ½ cup of rice onto each of 4 serving plates. Spoon ¼ of the chicken and ¼ of the spinach mixture over each serving. Drizzle with the vinegar and sprinkle with the chopped onion and bread crumbs. **Yield:** 4 (3 ounces chicken, 2½ cups spinach mixture and ½ cup rice) servings.

PER SERVING:
CALORIES: 302; CARBOHYDRATE: 36.4 g; PROTEIN: 25.3 g; TOTAL FAT: 6.7 g;
CHOLESTEROL: 60 mg; SODIUM: 333 mg; FIBER: 7 g;
CALORIES FROM FAT: 20%

Moroccan Chicken Tagine

5 teaspoons cumin seeds
5 teaspoons coriander seeds
2¹/2 teaspoons whole allspice
5 teaspoons nutmeg ♦ 2¹/2 teaspoons ginger
1¹/4 teaspoons red pepper
1¹/4 teaspoons cinnamon
1 teaspoon olive oil
8 cups vertically sliced onions (about 2 pounds)
¹/2 teaspoon salt ♦ 1¹/2 teaspoons sugar
¹/2 teaspoon black pepper
1 (10-ounce) can fat-free less-sodium chicken broth
4 boneless skinless chicken breasts
1 (15-ounce) can no-salt-added chick-peas or garbanzo beans, drained
¹/4 cup raisins
4 cups hot cooked couscous

Process the cumin seeds, coriander seeds and allspice in a spice grinder or coffee grinder until finely ground. Combine the cumin mixture, nutmeg, ginger, red pepper and cinnamon in a bowl and mix well; set aside. Heat the olive oil in a Dutch oven over medium heat. Add the onions and salt to the hot oil and mix well. Cook, covered, for 10 minutes, stirring occasionally. Add 1 teaspoon of the cumin mixture, sugar and black pepper to the onion mixture and mix well. Cook, covered, for 15 minutes, stirring occasionally. Stir in the broth. Cook for 30 minutes, stirring occasionally. Add the chicken, chick-peas and raisins and mix well. Bake, covered, at 375 degrees for 30 minutes. Serve with the couscous. Store the leftover cumin mixture in an airtight container for up to 6 months. **Yield:** 4 (1 chicken breast, ²/3 cup onion mixture and 1 cup couscous) servings.

Per Serving:
Calories: 543; Carbohydrate: 91.6 g; Protein: 31.1 g; Total Fat: 5 g;
Cholesterol: 58 mg; Sodium: 233 mg; Fiber: 10 g;
Calories from Fat: 8%

Traditions in
the Making

Paella Valenciana

3 (8-ounce) bottles clam juice ♦ 1/2 cup dry white wine
1/4 teaspoon saffron powder or turmeric
2 boneless skinless chicken breasts, cut into 1-inch pieces
1/4 teaspoon salt ♦ 3 tablespoons olive oil
4 ounces large shrimp, peeled and deveined
1/2 cup chopped green bell pepper ♦ 1/2 cup chopped red bell pepper
1/2 cup chopped onion ♦ 4 garlic cloves, minced
2 1/2 teaspoons smoked Spanish paprika or paprika
1/4 teaspoon crushed red pepper flakes ♦ 1 cup chopped tomato
1 1/2 cups short grain rice ♦ 8 ounces fresh clams, cleaned
1 pound small mussels, scrubbed and debearded

Bring the clam juice, wine and saffron powder to a simmer in a small saucepan; do not boil. Keep warm over low heat. Sprinkle the chicken with the salt. Heat 1 tablespoon of the olive oil in a paella pan or large ovenproof skillet over medium-high heat. Cook the chicken in the hot oil until brown on both sides. Remove the chicken to a bowl with a slotted spoon, reserving the pan drippings. Heat 1 tablespoon of the olive oil with the reserved pan drippings. Add the shrimp. Cook over high heat for 1 to 2 minutes or just until the shrimp begin to turn pink; do not overcook the shrimp as they will continue to cook in the paella. Remove the shrimp to a bowl using a slotted spoon, reserving the pan drippings.

Heat the remaining 1 tablespoon olive oil with the reserved pan drippings over medium-high heat. Stir in the bell peppers, onion, garlic, paprika and red pepper flakes. Sauté for 3 minutes. Stir in the tomato. Cook for 2 minutes. Add the rice and stir until coated. Stir in the warm clam juice mixture. Bring to a boil. Cook for 3 minutes. Stir in the chicken and shrimp. Cook for 2 minutes. Add the clams and mussels and mix well. Bake at 400 degrees for 15 to 20 minutes or until the clam shells and mussel shells open; discard any unopened shells. Let stand, covered, for 10 minutes before serving. **Yield:** 8 (1-cup) servings.

Per Serving:
Calories: 291; Carbohydrate: 33.8 g; Protein: 20 g; Total Fat: 7 g;
Cholesterol: 54.6 mg; Sodium: 396 mg; Fiber: 0.6 g;
Calories from Fat: 22%

Traditions in the Making

Mediterranean Lasagna

2 cups chopped leeks ♦ 1¹/2 cups chopped onions
3 garlic cloves, minced ♦ 1 teaspoon mint flakes
¹/2 teaspoon fennel seeds
1 (14-ounce) can artichoke hearts, rinsed, drained and coarsely chopped
1 medium red bell pepper, roasted and chopped
1 cup drained rinsed canned cannellini beans ♦ 1 tablespoon olive oil
2 tablespoons flour ♦ 1¹/2 cups fat-free milk
4 ounces feta cheese, crumbled
2 tablespoons grated Parmesan cheese ♦ 6 no-boil lasagna noodles
1 (10-ounce) package frozen chopped spinach, thawed and drained
³/4 cup (3 ounces) shredded part-skim mozzarella cheese
1 tablespoon grated Parmesan cheese

Sauté the leeks, onions, garlic, mint flakes and fennel seeds in a nonstick skillet sprayed with nonstick cooking spray for 5 minutes. Add the artichokes and bell pepper and mix well. Sauté for 3 minutes. Stir in the beans. Remove from the heat. Heat the olive oil in a saucepan over medium heat. Whisk in the flour. Cook for 2 minutes, whisking constantly. Add the fat-free milk gradually, whisking constantly. Cook for 4 minutes or until slightly thickened, whisking constantly. Remove from the heat. Add the feta cheese and 2 tablespoons Parmesan cheese and stir until blended.

Spread ¹/4 cup of the cheese sauce over the bottom of an 8×8-inch baking dish sprayed with nonstick cooking spray. Layer 2 of the noodles, ¹/2 of the leek mixture, ¹/2 of the spinach, ¹/4 cup of the mozzarella cheese and ¹/2 cup of the cheese sauce in the prepared baking dish. Top with 2 noodles, remaining leek mixture, remaining spinach, ¹/4 cup of the mozzarella cheese, ¹/2 cup of the cheese sauce and remaining 2 noodles. Spread the remaining cheese sauce over the top and sprinkle with the remaining ¹/4 cup mozzarella cheese and 1 tablespoon Parmesan cheese. Bake, covered, at 375 degrees for 35 minutes; remove the cover. Bake for 15 minutes longer or until golden brown and bubbly. Let stand for 5 minutes before serving. **Yield:** 6 servings.

Per Serving:
Calories: 341; Carbohydrate: 42.6 g; Protein: 18.8 g; Total Fat: 11.2 g;
Cholesterol: 45 mg; Sodium: 388 mg; Fiber: 4.4 g;
Calories from Fat: 30%

Traditions in
the Making

Whole Wheat Pizza Crust

2 teaspoons dry yeast

1 cup warm (105 to 115 degrees) water

1¹/4 cups unbleached all-purpose flour or bread flour

²/3 cup whole wheat flour

¹/4 cup rolled oats

2 tablespoons olive oil

2 tablespoons flaxseed, ground, or 3 tablespoons flaxseed meal

¹/2 teaspoon salt

TRADITIONS IN THE MAKING

PORTOBELLO AND ONION PIZZA

Toppings and Assembly

1 tablespoon olive oil ◆ 2 cups sliced white or yellow onions
¹/8 teaspoon salt ◆ Freshly ground pepper to taste
1 tablespoon olive oil
1 (6-ounce) package sliced portobello mushrooms, cut into quarters
1 (4-ounce) package sliced fresh mushrooms
1 large garlic clove, minced ◆ 2 tablespoons chopped fresh parsley
1 tablespoon fresh thyme leaves ◆ 1 tablespoon red wine vinegar
2 tablespoons freshly grated asiago cheese or Parmesan cheese

For the crust, dissolve the yeast in the warm water in a large bowl. Let stand for 5 minutes. Add 1 cup of the all-purpose flour, whole wheat flour, oats, olive oil, flaxseed and salt; stir until a soft dough forms. Knead the dough on a lightly floured surface for 8 to 10 minutes, adding enough of the remaining ¹/4 cup all-purpose flour 1 tablespoon at a time to make an easily handled dough. Place the dough in a bowl sprayed with nonstick cooking spray or coated with oil and turn to coat. Let rise, covered with plastic wrap, for 30 minutes or until doubled in bulk.

For the toppings, heat 1 tablespoon olive oil in a nonstick skillet over medium heat. Cook the onions in the hot oil for 5 minutes. Stir in the salt and pepper. Cook over low heat for 20 minutes or until the onions are caramelized. Remove the onions to a plate and cover to keep warm. Heat 1 tablespoon olive oil in the same skillet over medium-high heat. Sauté the mushrooms in the hot oil for 5 to 8 minutes or until light brown. Remove from the heat. Stir in the garlic, parsley, thyme and vinegar. Punch the dough down. Let rest, covered, for 5 minutes. Pat the dough over the bottom and up the side of a 12-inch pizza pan dusted with cornmeal. Crimp the edge to form a rim. Let rise, covered, for 10 minutes. Spread the onions to within ¹/2 inch of the edge. Top with the mushroom mixture and sprinkle with the cheese. Bake at 450 degrees for 10 minutes or until the crust is brown. **Yield:** 6 (1-wedge) servings.

PER SERVING:
CALORIES: 296; CARBOHYDRATE: 42 g; PROTEIN: 8.7 g; TOTAL FAT: 11.6 g;
CHOLESTEROL: 2 mg; SODIUM: 134 mg; FIBER: 4.7 g;
CALORIES FROM FAT: 35%

Muhammara

2 red bell peppers
2 (2-ounce) slices whole wheat nut bread, such as Arnold Health Nut
1 habanero chile, seeded
2 tablespoons water
3 garlic cloves
1 tablespoon olive oil
2 teaspoons balsamic vinegar
2 teaspoons pomegranate molasses or molasses
1 teaspoon cumin seeds
1/4 teaspoon crushed red pepper
1/4 teaspoon salt
1/3 cup walnuts, toasted

Cut the bell peppers lengthwise into halves. Discard the seeds and membranes. Arrange the bell pepper halves skin side up on a baking sheet lined with foil; flatten with hand. Broil for 15 minutes or until blackened. Place the bell pepper halves in a sealable plastic bag and seal tightly. Let stand for 20 minutes; remove the skins. Combine the bell peppers, bread, habanero chile, water, garlic, olive oil, vinegar, molasses, cumin seeds, red pepper and salt in a food processor. Process until smooth. Add the walnuts. Pulse 5 times or just until the walnuts are coarsely chopped. You may purchase pomegranate molasses at Middle Eastern markets. **Yield:** 16 (2-tablespoon) servings.

Per Serving:
Calories: 50; Carbohydrate: 5.4 g; Protein: 1.5 g; Total Fat: 2.7 g;
Cholesterol: 0 mg; Sodium: 74 mg; Fiber: 0.9 g;
Calories from Fat: 49%

Muhammara is a pepper purée which complements Spicy Kofte found on page 120 and Turkish Fish Sandwiches found on page 100. Although originally from southeast Turkey, muhammara has become widely used in Istanbul restaurants as a condiment with just about everything. It can also be served as a dip with pita bread or flatbread.

TRADITIONS IN
THE MAKING

TRADITIONS IN THE MAKING

STRAIGHT-FROM-ITALY TOMATO SAUCE

2 tablespoons olive oil
1 onion, finely chopped
3 garlic cloves, minced
1 (6-ounce) can tomato paste
1 (28-ounce) can crushed no-salt-added tomatoes
1/3 cup white wine
8 fresh basil leaves, or 1 tablespoon dried basil leaves
1/2 teaspoon oregano
1/4 teaspoon pepper
1/8 teaspoon salt
1/8 teaspoon sugar (optional)

Heat the olive oil in a saucepan over low to medium heat. Cook the onion and garlic in the hot oil for 5 to 7 minutes or until the onion is tender, stirring constantly; do not allow the onion to brown. Stir in the tomato paste. Add the undrained tomatoes and mix well. Stir in the wine, basil, oregano, pepper, salt and sugar. Simmer, covered, over low heat for about 45 minutes or to the desired consistency, stirring occasionally. Serve with 16 ounces hot cooked pasta. **Yield:** 8 (1/2-cup) servings.

PER SERVING:
CALORIES: 116; CARBOHYDRATE: 16.5 g; PROTEIN: 4.2 g; TOTAL FAT: 3.5 g;
CHOLESTEROL: 0 mg; SODIUM: 128 mg; FIBER: 3.2 g;
CALORIES FROM FAT: 27%

SICILIAN-STYLE PASTA SAUCE

1 teaspoon olive oil
8 ounces ultra-lean ground beef
1 cup chopped onion
4 garlic cloves, minced
2 (14-ounce) cans diced no-salt-added tomatoes
1/2 cup dry red wine, or 2 tablespoons balsamic vinegar
2 tablespoons tomato paste
1 tablespoon sugar
1 tablespoon chopped fresh basil, or 1 teaspoon dried basil
1/2 teaspoon Italian seasoning
1/4 teaspoon pepper
2 tablespoons chopped fresh parsley

Heat the olive oil in a saucepan or skillet over medium-high heat. Sauté the ground beef, onion and garlic in the hot oil for 5 minutes or until the ground beef is no longer pink. Stir in the undrained tomatoes, wine, tomato paste, sugar, basil, Italian seasoning and pepper. Bring to a boil; reduce the heat to medium. Cook for 15 minutes, stirring occasionally. Stir in the parsley. Serve over your favorite hot cooked pasta. **Yield:** 4 (1-cup) servings.

PER SERVING:
CALORIES: 187; CARBOHYDRATE: 20.2 g; PROTEIN: 15.2 g; TOTAL FAT: 5.9 g; CHOLESTEROL: 35 mg; SODIUM: 168 mg; FIBER: 3 g; CALORIES FROM FAT: 28%

Waist-to-Hip Ratio helps you understand your distribution of fat. Measure your waist at the navel, and then measure your hips at the widest area around the buttocks. Divide the waist by the hips. This is the Waist-to-Hip Ratio.

For men, increased risk for coronary heart disease occurs at ratios greater than 0.95.

For women, increased risk for coronary heart disease occurs at ratios greater than 0.86.

TRADITIONS IN
THE MAKING

APPETIZERS SOUPS AND SALADS

A ppetizers combine two important features of the Mediterranean diet: smaller portions and more time for socializing. Appetizers go by many names in the region: meza, tapas, antipasto, merende, hors d'oeuvre. In Greece, they are called mezethes, which means "middle," because they are typically eaten between meals during the middle of the day.

The traditions of the Mediterranean table flow in the form of coffee, tea, juices, and wine. Beverages play a major role, from those accompanying lavish meals to those shared by friends at the local coffee shop.

Soups or sopas from this region often feature fresh vegetables that are mainstays of the diet. In Malta, minestra or minestrone is a beloved thick vegetable soup and lentil soup is a favorite in the Middle East.

In the Mediterranean, salads are served at the end of the meal, rather than the beginning. Their leafy dark green textures are a far cry from iceberg lettuce and fit beautifully into a well-balanced, heart healthy diet.

The recipes featured in this chapter for appetizers, soups, salads, and beverages capture the best and healthiest of these Mediterranean favorites. They might just become the beginning, middle, or end of your favorite meals.

In many Mediterranean countries, hosts delight in a table laden with appetizers as a symbol of abundance and hospitality. The French call appetizers hors d'oeuvres. The Italians call them antipasti. These tasty tidbits are called tapas in Spain, while the Middle Eastern countries refer to them as mezes. No matter what name you choose to call them, appetizers are an interesting way to start a meal. Or choose several and make them your entrée.

APPETIZERS, SOUPS AND SALADS

ANTIPASTO SALSA

1 cup chopped tomato ◆ 1 cup chopped zucchini
1/2 cup chopped drained canned artichoke hearts
1/2 cup chopped fresh basil
1/3 cup bottled chopped roasted red bell peppers
1/4 cup minced onion
2 tablespoons chopped pitted kalamata olives
1 tablespoon balsamic vinegar ◆ 1 teaspoon olive oil

Combine all the ingredients in a bowl and toss to mix. Chill, covered, until serving time. **Yield:** 6 (1/2-cup) servings.

PER SERVING:
CALORIES: 32; CARBOHYDRATE: 5.2 g; PROTEIN: 1.3 g; TOTAL FAT: 1.2 g;
CHOLESTEROL: 0 mg; SODIUM: 80 mg; FIBER: 0.8 g;
CALORIES FROM FAT: 34%

TOMATO BASIL BRUSCHETTA

4 ripe plum tomatoes, finely chopped
1/4 cup coarsely chopped fresh basil ◆ 1 tablespoon finely minced garlic
2 tablespoons finely chopped fresh Italian parsley
2 teaspoons lemon juice ◆ 1/8 teaspoon crushed red pepper flakes
Salt and freshly ground black pepper to taste
8 (1/4-inch-thick) slices French or Italian bread
2 garlic cloves, cut into halves

Toss the first 8 ingredients in a bowl. Let stand, covered, at room temperature for 3 hours or longer, stirring occasionally. Grill or toast the bread slices just before serving time. Rub 1 side of each bread slice with the garlic halves. Spoon some of the tomato mixture on top of each toasted bread slice. **Yield:** 8 (1-slice) servings.

PER SERVING:
CALORIES: 141; CARBOHYDRATE: 27 g; PROTEIN: 5 g; TOTAL FAT: 1.3 g;
CHOLESTEROL: 0 mg; SODIUM: 274 mg; FIBER: 0.7 g;
CALORIES FROM FAT: 8%

GOAT CHEESE- AND WALNUT-STUFFED ENDIVE

$^{1}/3$ cup coarsely chopped walnuts
2 tablespoons honey
$^{1}/4$ cup balsamic vinegar
3 tablespoons orange juice
16 small navel orange sections (about 2 oranges)
16 Belgian endive spears (about 2 heads)
$^{1}/4$ cup (1 ounce) crumbled goat cheese or blue cheese
1 tablespoon minced fresh chives
$^{1}/4$ teaspoon cracked pepper

Combine the walnuts and 1 tablespoon of the honey in a small bowl and mix well. Spread the walnut mixture on a baking sheet sprayed with nonstick cooking spray. Bake at 350 degrees for 5 minutes and stir. Bake for 5 minutes longer. Combine the remaining 1 tablespoon honey, vinegar and orange juice in a small saucepan and mix well. Bring to a boil over high heat. Boil for 5 minutes or until the mixture is reduced to 3 tablespoons, stirring occasionally. Place 1 orange section on each endive spear. Top each orange section with 1 teaspoon of the cheese and 1 teaspoon of the walnut mixture. Arrange the stuffed endive spears on a serving platter and drizzle with the vinegar mixture. Sprinkle with the chives and cracked pepper. **Yield:** 8 (2-stuffed endive spear) servings.

PER SERVING:
CALORIES: 86; CARBOHYDRATE: 11.9 g; PROTEIN: 2.1 g; TOTAL FAT: 3.9 g;
CHOLESTEROL: 1.6 mg; SODIUM: 20 mg; FIBER: 2 g;
CALORIES FROM FAT: 40%

The origins of eating mezes in Turkey are thought to date back to the 1500s when the sultan used tasters to test his food for poison. The tasters were given small plates of food samples. The wealthy class copied this practice and made it fashionable. Eventually, mezes became part of the Turkish culture.

APPETIZERS, SOUPS
AND SALADS

Tomato- and Pesto-Stuffed Mushrooms

24 large fresh mushrooms
15 sun-dried tomatoes
3/4 cup boiling water
1 cup nonfat sour cream
1/3 cup nonfat cream cheese, softened
1/4 cup minced fresh basil
1/4 cup minced pecans, toasted
1 garlic clove, minced
1/4 cup fine dry bread crumbs

Wipe the mushrooms with damp paper towels. Remove the stems and reserve for another use. Heat a nonstick skillet sprayed with olive oil-flavor nonstick cooking spray over medium-high heat. Add the mushroom caps to the hot skillet. Sauté for 10 minutes. Remove the mushroom caps to paper towels to drain. Combine the sun-dried tomatoes and boiling water in a heatproof bowl. Let stand, covered, for 15 minutes to reconstitute. Drain and finely chop the sun-dried tomatoes.

Combine the sun-dried tomatoes, sour cream, cream cheese, basil, pecans and garlic in a bowl and mix well. Spoon 1 heaping tablespoon of the tomato mixture into each mushroom cap and sprinkle each with 1/2 teaspoon of the bread crumbs. Arrange the mushroom caps stuffing side up on a baking sheet sprayed with olive oil-flavor nonstick cooking spray. Bake at 375 degrees for 10 to 15 minutes or until heated through.
Yield: 24 (1-mushroom) servings.

PER SERVING:
CALORIES: 35; CARBOHYDRATE: 4.3 g; PROTEIN: 2.2 g; TOTAL FAT: 1.1 g;
CHOLESTEROL: 1 mg; SODIUM: 73 mg; FIBER: 0.4 g;
CALORIES FROM FAT: 28%

APPETIZERS, SOUPS
AND SALADS

Greek Spinach Pies
(Spanakopita)

2 (10-ounce) packages frozen chopped spinach,
thawed and drained ♦ 1 cup minced onion
2/3 cup crumbled feta cheese
2/3 cup part-skim ricotta cheese ♦ 1 teaspoon oregano
1/2 teaspoon garlic powder ♦ 1/2 teaspoon salt
1/2 teaspoon freshly ground pepper
14 sheets frozen phyllo pastry, thawed

Press the spinach between layers of paper towels until barely moist. Heat a large nonstick skillet sprayed with butter-flavor nonstick cooking spray over medium-high heat. Add the onion to the hot skillet. Sauté until tender. Remove from the heat. Stir in the spinach, feta cheese, ricotta cheese, oregano, garlic powder, salt and pepper. Place 1 of the pastry sheets on a damp paper towel, keeping the remaining pastry covered with a damp tea towel to prevent drying out. Coat the pastry sheet lightly with butter-flavor nonstick cooking spray. Layer the pastry with a second pastry sheet and lightly spray with butter-flavor nonstick cooking spray. Cut the stack of pastry sheets crosswise into seven 2 1/3-inch strips.

Working with 1 strip at a time, place approximately 2 teaspoons of the spinach mixture at the base of each strip, keeping the remaining strips covered with a damp tea towel. Fold the right bottom corner over to form a triangle. Continue folding the triangle back and forth to the end of the strip. Arrange the triangles seam side down on a baking sheet sprayed with butter-flavor nonstick cooking spray. Repeat this process with the remaining 12 sheets of phyllo pastry and remaining spinach mixture. Spray the tops of the triangles lightly with butter-flavor nonstick cooking spray. Bake at 350 degrees for 25 minutes or until golden brown. Serve immediately. **Yield:** 49 (1-pastry) servings.

PER SERVING:
CALORIES: 34; CARBOHYDRATE: 3.9 g; PROTEIN: 1.5 g; TOTAL FAT: 1.3 g;
CHOLESTEROL: 3 mg; SODIUM: 86 mg; FIBER: 0.4 g;
CALORIES FROM FAT: 34%

Spanakopita is a classic Mediterranean recipe from Greece. These appetizer-size spanakopitas are spinach-filled phyllo pockets.

APPETIZERS, SOUPS AND SALADS

FAUX CHAMPAGNE

4 cups apple juice, chilled
2 cups lemon-lime soda, chilled
Orange slices (optional)
Sprigs of fresh mint (optional)

Mix the apple juice and soda in a pitcher. Garnish each serving with an orange slice and sprig of mint. Serve in Champagne flutes.
Yield: 6 (1-cup) servings.

PER SERVING:
CALORIES: 110; CARBOHYDRATE: 27.3 g; PROTEIN: .06 g; TOTAL FAT: 0.2 g;
CHOLESTEROL: 0 mg; SODIUM: 11.8 mg; FIBER: TRACE g;
CALORIES FROM FAT: <2%

FRUIT JUICE SPRITZER

1 (6-ounce) can frozen orange juice concentrate, thawed
1 (6-ounce) can frozen apple juice concentrate, thawed
4 1/2 cups club soda, chilled
Orange slices (optional)

Combine the orange juice concentrate, apple juice concentrate and club soda in a pitcher and stir until blended. Pour over ice in glasses. Garnish each serving with an orange slice. **Yield:** 6 (1-cup) servings.

PER SERVING:
CALORIES: 92; CARBOHYDRATE: 22.4 g; PROTEIN: 0.8 g; TOTAL FAT: 0.2 g;
CHOLESTEROL: 0 mg; SODIUM: 44 mg; FIBER: 0.2 g;
CALORIES FROM FAT: 2%

Sangria

1 (25-ounce) bottle burgundy or other dry red wine, chilled
1/2 cup sugar ◆ 1 orange, thinly sliced
1 lemon or lime, thinly sliced
1 (10-ounce) can lemon-lime soda
1/2 cup club soda

Combine the wine, sugar, orange slices and lemon slices in a large pitcher and stir until the sugar dissolves. Add the lemon-lime soda and club soda just before serving and stir to blend. Pour over ice in glasses. **Yield:** 8 (3/4-cup) servings.

Per Serving:
Calories: 140; Carbohydrate: 20.6 g; Protein: 0.4 g; Total Fat: 0 g;
Cholesterol: 0 mg; Sodium: 14 mg; Fiber: 0.6 g;
Calories from Fat: 0%

Spiced Iced Tea

16 cups water ◆ 1 teaspoon cardamom seeds
1 teaspoon whole allspice
3 (3-inch) cinnamon sticks, broken into halves
8 tea bags ◆ Sprigs of fresh mint (optional)

Combine the water, cardamom seeds, allspice and cinnamon sticks in a large heavy saucepan. Bring to a boil; remove from the heat. Add the tea bags to the spice mixture. Steep, covered, for 5 minutes. Strain the tea into a heatproof pitcher. Chill until serving time. Pour the tea over ice in glasses. Garnish each serving with a sprig of mint. **Yield:** 16 (1-cup) servings.

Per Serving:
Calories: 2; Carbohydrate: 0.6 g; Protein: 0.1 g; Total Fat: 0 g;
Cholesterol: 0 mg; Sodium: 0 mg; Fiber: trace g;
Calories from Fat: 0%

Appetizers, Soups and Salads

Greek coffee is a very fine grind, almost a powder, and is available in Middle Eastern markets or wherever Greek groceries are sold. Coffee is prepared in a similar manner in other regions of the Mediterranean, especially Turkey and the Middle Eastern countries. Depending on the region, this coffee could be called Turkish or Arabic coffee.

APPETIZERS, SOUPS
AND SALADS

MOROCCAN MINT TEA

2¹/₂ cups boiling water ♦ 2 teaspoons sugar
2 teaspoons loose green tea leaves, or 2 green tea bags
6 fresh mint leaves, crushed

Mix the boiling water, sugar, tea leaves and mint in a heatproof bowl. Steep for 5 minutes. Strain the tea through a fine sieve into mugs, discarding the solids. **Yield:** 2 (1-cup) servings.

PER SERVING:
CALORIES: 17; CARBOHYDRATE: 4.2 g; PROTEIN: 0 g; TOTAL FAT: 0 g;
CHOLESTEROL: 0 mg; SODIUM: 0 mg; FIBER: 0 g;
CALORIES FROM FAT: 0%

GREEK COFFEE

2/3 cup cold water ♦ 2 teaspoons sugar
2 teaspoons (heaping) Greek or Turkish coffee

Bring the cold water and sugar to a boil in a small saucepan. Remove from the heat and stir in the coffee vigorously with a spoon. Return the saucepan to the heat. The coffee will boil almost to the top immediately and have a brown foam on top. Just before the coffee overflows, remove from the heat and tap the side of the saucepan with a spoon until the foam subsides a bit. Return the saucepan to the heat. Bring the coffee to a boil almost to the top. Remove from the heat and tap the saucepan 3 times with a spoon. Return the saucepan to the heat for the third time and allow the coffee to almost overflow again. Quickly remove from the heat. Spoon the foam evenly into 2 demitasse cups and then slowly fill the cups with the coffee, being careful not to disturb the foam on top of each cup. Serve immediately. **Yield:** 2 servings.

PER SERVING:
CALORIES: 15; CARBOHYDRATE: 4 g; PROTEIN: 0 g; TOTAL FAT: 0 g;
CHOLESTEROL: 0 mg; SODIUM: 0 mg; FIBER: 0 g;
CALORIES FROM FAT: 0%

ALMOND CAPPUCCINO

2 cups fat-free milk
1 vanilla bean, split, or 1 teaspoon vanilla extract
2 tablespoons instant espresso granules
1/8 teaspoon almond extract ♦ 1/4 teaspoon baking cocoa

Combine the fat-free milk and vanilla bean in a medium saucepan. Cook over low heat until bubbly. Stir in the espresso granules and remove from the heat. Discard the vanilla bean. Stir in the flavoring. Pour 1 cup of the milk mixture into a blender and process until frothy. Pour into a mug and sprinkle with 1/8 teaspoon of the baking cocoa. Repeat the process with the remaining milk mixture and remaining baking cocoa. **Yield:** 2 (1-cup) servings.

PER SERVING:
CALORIES: 96; CARBOHYDRATE: 13.4 g; PROTEIN: 8.8 g; TOTAL FAT: 0.5 g;
CHOLESTEROL: 5 mg; SODIUM: 129 mg; FIBER: 0.1 g;
CALORIES FROM FAT: 5%

ESPRESSO AU LAIT

1/4 cup packed brown sugar
1/4 cup instant espresso granules ♦ 1 3/4 cups water
1 3/4 cups 1% milk ♦ Orange zest (optional)

Combine the brown sugar and espresso granules in a 1-quart microwave-safe measuring cup. Stir in the water and milk. Microwave, uncovered, on High for 5 minutes or until heated through, stirring every 2 minutes. Pour into mugs and garnish with orange zest. **Yield:** 4 (1-cup) servings.

PER SERVING:
CALORIES: 102; CARBOHYDRATE: 20 g; PROTEIN: 3.7 g; TOTAL FAT: 1 g;
CHOLESTEROL: 4.3 mg; SODIUM: 53 mg; FIBER: 0.1 g;
CALORIES FROM FAT: 9%

Instant espresso powder is located with the instant coffees in large supermarkets and gourmet coffee shops. You may substitute two teaspoons instant coffee granules for each teaspoon of instant espresso powder.

APPETIZERS, SOUPS AND SALADS

Carrot Soup

4 cups low-sodium vegetable juice cocktail
4 large carrots, peeled and sliced
1 medium onion, chopped
2 ribs celery, chopped
1 large garlic clove, minced
Pepper to taste
1/2 teaspoon dill weed, basil or thyme
1/8 to 1/4 teaspoon salt (optional)
1/4 cup nonfat sour cream

Combine the vegetable juice cocktail, carrots, onion, celery, garlic and pepper in a 2-quart saucepan. Bring to a boil; reduce the heat. Simmer until the carrots are tender, stirring occasionally. Process the carrot mixture in a blender or food processor until puréed. Return the purée to the saucepan. Stir in the dill weed and salt. Simmer just until heated through, stirring frequently. Ladle into soup bowls. Top each serving with 1 tablespoon of the sour cream. The recipe was calculated without the addition of the salt. If 1/8 teaspoon salt is added to the soup, the sodium content will be increased to 271 milligrams per serving. If 1/4 teaspoon of salt is added, the sodium content will be increased to 343 milligrams per serving. **Yield:** 4 (1-cup) servings.

Per Serving:
Calories: 114; Carbohydrate: 25.5 g; Protein: 3.3 g; Total Fat: 0.2 g;
Cholesterol: 2.5 mg; Sodium: 199 mg; Fiber: 4.8 g;
Calories from Fat: 2%

MEDITERRANEAN CHICK-PEA, TOMATO AND PASTA SOUP

2 teaspoons olive oil
1 cup chopped onion
1 (16-ounce) can fat-free less-sodium chicken broth
1 (15-ounce) can chick-peas or garbanzo beans, drained
1 (14-ounce) can diced no-salt-added tomatoes
1¹/2 cups water
1/2 teaspoon cumin
1/4 teaspoon cinnamon
1/4 teaspoon pepper
1/2 cup ditalini
2 tablespoons chopped fresh parsley

Heat the olive oil in a large saucepan over medium-high heat. Sauté the onion in the hot oil for 3 minutes or until tender. Stir in the broth, chick-peas, undrained tomatoes, water, cumin, cinnamon and pepper. Bring to a boil; reduce the heat. Simmer, covered, for 5 minutes, stirring occasionally. Add the pasta and mix well. Cook for 9 minutes or until the pasta is tender, stirring occasionally. Stir in the parsley. Ladle into soup bowls. **Yield:** 4 (1¹/2-cup) servings.

PER SERVING:
CALORIES: 242; CARBOHYDRATE: 39.9 g; PROTEIN: 11.4 g; TOTAL FAT: 4.7 g;
CHOLESTEROL: 0 mg; SODIUM: 280 mg; FIBER: 4.6 g;
CALORIES FROM FAT: 17%

APPETIZERS, SOUPS
AND SALADS

GREEK EGG LEMON SOUP
(AVGOLEMONO)

2 (16-ounce) cans fat-free less-sodium chicken broth
1 egg
1/2 cup egg substitute
1/3 cup fresh lemon juice
1 teaspoon grated lemon zest (optional)
1/8 teaspoon red pepper, or to taste
1 cup cooked brown rice or white rice
1/4 cup chopped fresh parsley
Thin lemon slices (optional)

Bring the broth to a boil in a saucepan over medium-high heat. Reduce the heat and let the broth simmer. Whisk the egg and egg substitute in a bowl until blended. Beat in the lemon juice, lemon zest and red pepper. Add 1 ladle of the hot broth to the egg mixture gradually, stirring constantly. Whisk the egg mixture into the hot broth. Cook over low heat for 5 minutes or just until thickened, stirring constantly; do not boil. Divide the rice evenly among 4 soup bowls. Ladle the soup over the rice and sprinkle with the parsley. Garnish with lemon slices.
Yield: 4 (1 cup soup and 1/4 cup rice) servings.

PER SERVING:
CALORIES: 109; CARBOHYDRATE: 14.8 g; PROTEIN: 8 g; TOTAL FAT: 1.7 g;
CHOLESTEROL: 58 mg; SODIUM: 458 mg; FIBER: 1 g;
CALORIES FROM FAT: 14%

Harira

1 1/4 pounds boneless leg of lamb, trimmed and
cut into 1-inch cubes
1/4 teaspoon salt ◆ 1/4 teaspoon black pepper
1 tablespoon olive oil
1 cup chopped onion
1 tablespoon no-salt-added tomato paste
4 cups water
1 cup drained canned no-salt-added chick-peas or garbanzo beans
1/2 teaspoon cinnamon ◆ 1/4 teaspoon red pepper
2 cups chopped tomatoes
1/2 cup dried small red lentils or brown lentils, sorted and rinsed
1/2 cup chopped red bell pepper
1/2 cup hot cooked angel hair pasta (about 1 ounce uncooked pasta)
1 tablespoon minced fresh cilantro
1 tablespoon fresh lemon juice

Sprinkle the lamb with the salt and pepper. Heat the olive oil in a large Dutch oven over high heat. Cook the lamb in the hot oil for 5 minutes or until brown on all sides, stirring frequently. Stir in the onion. Cook for 1 minute, stirring frequently. Add the tomato paste and mix well. Cook for 1 minute, stirring frequently. Stir in the water, chick-peas, cinnamon and red pepper. Bring to a boil; reduce the heat. Simmer for 30 minutes, stirring occasionally. Stir in the tomatoes, lentils and bell pepper. Bring to a boil; reduce the heat. Simmer for 30 minutes or until the lentils are tender, stirring occasionally. Stir in the pasta, cilantro and lemon juice. Cook for 1 minute or just until heated through, stirring frequently. Ladle into soup bowls. **Yield:** 4 (1 1/4-cup) servings.

PER SERVING:
CALORIES: 359; CARBOHYDRATE: 40.6 g; PROTEIN: 30.4 g; TOTAL FAT: 9.2 g;
CHOLESTEROL: 55 mg; SODIUM: 235 mg; FIBER: 6.8 g;
CALORIES FROM FAT: 23%

Traditionally, Harira is eaten to break the daily fast during the Muslim month of Ramadan. If preferred, lean beef can be substituted for the lamb.

APPETIZERS, SOUPS
AND SALADS

Italian Minestrone

8 ounces dried red kidney beans or Great Northern beans
1 tablespoon olive oil ♦ 1 cup chopped onion
1 cup chopped carrots ♦ 1/2 cup sliced celery
2 tablespoons minced fresh parsley
1 tablespoon minced garlic
1 tablespoon whole basil ♦ 1/2 teaspoon whole thyme
1/2 teaspoon whole oregano
1/4 teaspoon salt ♦ 1/8 teaspoon red pepper ♦ 4 cups water
2 (16-ounce) cans fat-free less-sodium chicken broth
1 cup frozen Italian green beans
2 (14-ounce) cans no-salt-added whole tomatoes, coarsely chopped
2 cups coarsely shredded cabbage
1 1/2 cups thinly sliced zucchini
1 1/2 cups fresh spinach, coarsely chopped
1 cup elbow macaroni, ditalini or small shells
1/4 cup freshly grated Parmesan cheese or Romano cheese

Sort and rinse the beans and place in a large bowl. Add enough water to cover the beans by 2 inches. Soak for 8 to 10 hours; drain. Heat the olive oil in a Dutch oven over medium-high heat. Sauté the onion, carrots, celery, parsley and garlic in the hot oil until the onion and carrots are tender. Stir in the basil, thyme, oregano, salt and red pepper. Sauté for 1 minute. Add the kidney beans, 4 cups water, broth and Italian green beans. Bring to a boil; reduce the heat. Simmer, covered, for 1 hour or until the kidney beans are tender, stirring occasionally. Stir in the undrained tomatoes, cabbage, zucchini, spinach and pasta. Bring to a boil; reduce the heat. Simmer for 15 minutes, stirring occasionally. Ladle into soup bowls. Top each serving with 1 teaspoon of the cheese. **Yield:** 12 (1-cup) servings.

Per Serving:
Calories: 177; Carbohydrate: 29.6 g; Protein: 9.2 g; Total Fat: 2.6 g;
Cholesterol: 2 mg; Sodium: 252 mg; Fiber: 8 g;
Calories from Fat: 13%

**Appetizers, Soups
and Salads**

Pasta e Fagioli

1 pound dried navy beans ◆ 1 tablespoon olive oil
1 cup chopped onion ◆ 1/2 cup sliced carrots
1/2 cup chopped celery ◆ 2 garlic cloves, crushed
1 (28-ounce) can diced tomatoes
9 cups water ◆ 1/4 teaspoon crushed red pepper
1 bay leaf ◆ 2 garlic cloves, crushed
1 teaspoon oregano ◆ 1/2 teaspoon thyme
1/4 teaspoon rosemary ◆ 1/8 teaspoon salt
3/4 cup ditalini ◆ 1 cup chopped fresh flat-leaf parsley
1/4 teaspoon black pepper
3/4 cup (3 ounces) freshly grated Parmesan cheese

Sort and rinse the beans and place in a Dutch oven. Add enough water to cover the beans by 2 inches. Bring to a boil. Boil for 2 minutes and remove from the heat. Let stand, covered, for 1 hour. Drain the beans in a colander. Heat the olive oil in the Dutch oven over medium heat. Sauté the onion, carrots and celery in the hot oil for 5 minutes or until the vegetables are tender. Stir in 2 crushed garlic cloves. Cook for 1 minute, stirring frequently. Add the undrained tomatoes and mix well. Bring to a boil; reduce the heat. Simmer, covered, for 10 minutes, stirring occasionally. Add 9 cups water, red pepper and bay leaf and mix well. Simmer covered, for 1 hour and 50 minutes. Stir in 2 crushed garlic cloves, oregano, thyme, rosemary and salt. Simmer, covered, for 25 minutes or until the beans are tender, stirring occasionally. Discard the bay leaf.

Process 2 cups of the bean mixture in a food processor until puréed. Return the bean purée to the Dutch oven and mix well. Stir in the pasta. Cook for 7 minutes or until the pasta is tender, stirring occasionally. Remove from the heat. Stir in the parsley and black pepper. Ladle into soup bowls and sprinkle with the cheese. **Yield:** 8 (1 1/2 cups soup and 1 1/2 tablespoons cheese) servings.

PER SERVING:
CALORIES: 339; CARBOHYDRATE: 54.6 g; PROTEIN: 19.8 g; TOTAL FAT: 5.5 g;
CHOLESTEROL: 7 mg; SODIUM: 375 mg; FIBER: 8.7 g;
CALORIES FROM FAT: 15%

APPETIZERS, SOUPS
AND SALADS

Greek Chicken Salad

3 cups chopped cooked chicken breasts (about 12 ounces)
1 cup chopped seeded peeled cucumber
1/4 cup (1 ounce) crumbled feta cheese
1/4 cup chopped red onion
1/4 cup chopped fresh parsley
2 tablespoons sliced pitted kalamata olives
3/4 cup plain fat-free yogurt
1/2 cup fat-free mayonnaise
1 tablespoon oregano
3 garlic cloves, minced
4 (6-inch) pita rounds, cut into halves
8 Boston lettuce leaves

Combine the chicken, cucumber, cheese, onion, parsley and olives in a bowl and mix well. Combine the yogurt, mayonnaise, oregano and garlic in a small bowl and mix well. Add the yogurt mixture to the chicken mixture and toss to coat. Chill, covered, for 2 hours. Line each pita half with 1 lettuce leaf. Fill each half with 1/2 cup of the chicken salad. **Yield:** 8 servings.

Per Serving:
Calories: 185; Carbohydrate: 22.3 g; Protein: 18.3 g; Total Fat: 2 g;
Cholesterol: 39.9 mg; Sodium: 376 mg; Fiber: 1.2 g;
Calories from Fat: 10%

Salade Niçoise

2 (8-ounce) tuna steaks
3 tablespoons fresh lemon juice
Freshly ground pepper to taste
10 petite red potatoes
8 ounces green beans, trimmed
8 cups torn romaine
3 tomatoes, each cut into 6 wedges
3 hard-cooked eggs, sliced lengthwise into quarters
1 small green bell pepper, julienned
1/2 cup niçoise olives
2 tablespoons drained capers

Arrange the tuna in a shallow dish. Drizzle with the lemon juice and sprinkle with pepper. Marinate, covered, in the refrigerator for 15 minutes; drain. Arrange the tuna on a grill rack or broiler rack sprayed with nonstick cooking spray. Grill or broil for 4 minutes per side or until medium-well. Break the tuna into chunks. Steam the potatoes in a vegetable steamer for 7 minutes. Add the green beans. Steam, covered, for 8 minutes or until the potatoes are tender and the green beans are tender-crisp. Let stand until cool. Line a large serving platter with the lettuce. Arrange the tuna, potatoes, green beans, tomatoes, eggs and bell pepper in a decorative pattern over the lettuce. Top with the olives and capers. Serve with vinaigrette dressing. **Yield:** 6 servings.

Per Serving:
Calories: 287; Carbohydrate: 22 g; Protein: 28.8 g; Total Fat: 9.7 g;
Cholesterol: 61 mg; Sodium: 311 mg; Fiber: 4.5 g;
Calories from Fat: 31%

Salads can be much more delicious when a variety of interesting lettuces are used. Many grocery stores now carry a wide selection. Try arugula, escarole, endive, romaine, and Batavia lettuce in new salad creations. A variety of colors and textures can transform a so-so salad into a spectacular one.

Appetizers, Soups and Salads

GREEK SALAD WITH BROILED SHRIMP

12 medium shrimp
2 garlic cloves, minced
1/4 teaspoon pepper
1/8 teaspoon salt
1/4 cup fresh lemon juice
1/2 teaspoon oregano
1/4 teaspoon pepper
1/8 teaspoon salt
1 tablespoon olive oil
1 head romaine, cut crosswise into 1-inch strips
1 large tomato, cut into wedges
2 small cucumbers, coarsely chopped
1 small red onion, thinly sliced
2 tablespoons kalamata olives or black olives

Peel and devein the shrimp, leaving the tails intact. Toss the shrimp with the garlic, 1/4 teaspoon pepper and 1/8 teaspoon salt in a bowl. Thread 3 shrimp onto a skewer and arrange the skewer on a baking sheet. Repeat the process with the remaining shrimp and 3 more skewers. Spray the shrimp with garlic-flavor nonstick cooking spray. Broil for 2 to 3 minutes or until brown; turn. Broil until the shrimp turn pink. Whisk the lemon juice, oregano, 1/4 teaspoon pepper and 1/8 teaspoon salt in a bowl. Add the olive oil gradually, whisking constantly. Toss the romaine, tomato, cucumbers, onion and olives in a large salad bowl. Drizzle with the dressing and toss to coat. Divide the salad evenly among 4 serving plates. Top each serving with a shrimp skewer. **Yield:** 4 (2 cups salad and 3 shrimp) servings.

PER SERVING:
CALORIES: 103; CARBOHYDRATE: 9.3 g; PROTEIN: 7.3 g; TOTAL FAT: 5 g;
CHOLESTEROL: 32.3 mg; SODIUM: 248 mg; FIBER: 3.3 g;
CALORIES FROM FAT: 44%

APPETIZERS, SOUPS
AND SALADS

Arugula, Fig
and Blue Cheese Salad

2 cups torn red leaf lettuce
1 1/4 cups fresh figs, cut into quarters
1 cup trimmed arugula
2 tablespoons fresh lemon juice
2 teaspoons olive oil
1/8 teaspoon salt
1/4 teaspoon freshly ground pepper
3 tablespoons crumbled blue cheese

Toss the lettuce, figs and arugula in a salad bowl. Whisk the lemon juice, olive oil, salt and pepper in a bowl until blended. Drizzle the lemon juice mixture over the lettuce mixture and toss gently. Sprinkle with the cheese. **Yield:** 4 (1-cup) servings.

PER SERVING:
CALORIES: 74; CARBOHYDRATE: 11.6 g; PROTEIN: 2 g; TOTAL FAT: 2.9 g;
CHOLESTEROL: 4 mg; SODIUM: 152 mg; FIBER: 2.3 g;
CALORIES FROM FAT: 35%

Figs are abundant in the Mediterranean region and they give the Arugula, Fig and Blue Cheese Salad a hint of sweetness that accentuates the cheese. You may substitute Parmesan cheese shavings for the blue cheese.

APPETIZERS, SOUPS
AND SALADS

Tomatoes with Mozzarella and Basil
(Insalata Caprese)

4 large summer tomatoes
4 ounces fresh or part-skim mozzarella cheese
15 to 18 fresh basil leaves ♦ 1/8 teaspoon salt
Freshly ground pepper to taste ♦ 1 tablespoon extra-virgin olive oil
1 teaspoon red wine vinegar

Core the tomatoes and cut into 1/2-inch-thick wedges. Cut the mozzarella into 1/8- to 1/4-inch-thick slices. Alternate the tomato wedges, cheese slices and basil leaves slightly overlapping on a serving platter. Sprinkle with the salt and pepper. Mix the olive oil and vinegar in a bowl with a fork. Drizzle the olive oil mixture over the salad. Serve immediately. **Yield:** 6 servings.

Per Serving:
Calories: 87; Carbohydrate: 4.5 g; Protein: 5.3 g; Total Fat: 5.6 g;
Cholesterol: 10.6 mg; Sodium: 143 mg; Fiber: 1 g;
Calories from Fat: 58%

Yogurt and Cucumber Salad

2 garlic cloves ♦ 1/8 teaspoon salt
2 cups plain nonfat yogurt
1/2 large cucumber or 1 medium cucumber, peeled and coarsely chopped
1 teaspoon olive oil ♦ Finely chopped fresh mint

Mash the garlic with the salt using a mortar and pestle. Combine the garlic mixture, yogurt and cucumber in a bowl and mix gently. Drizzle with the olive oil and sprinkle with mint. **Yield:** 4 servings.

Per Serving:
Calories: 79; Carbohydrate: 10.9 g; Protein: 5.9 g; Total Fat: 1.2 g;
Cholesterol: 5 mg; Sodium: 141 mg; Fiber: trace g;
Calories from Fat: 14%

Appetizers, Soups
and Salads

86

TUSCANY BREAD SALAD
(TUSCAN PANZANELLA)

Red Wine Vinaigrette
3 tablespoons red wine vinegar
1 tablespoon water
1 tablespoon extra-virgin olive oil
3 garlic cloves, minced
1/2 teaspoon freshly ground pepper
1/8 teaspoon salt

Salad
4 (1-ounce) slices Italian bread, crusts trimmed
2 pounds ripe tomatoes, cut into 1-inch pieces
1 (15-ounce) can no-salt-added organic cannellini beans or
other white beans, drained
1 cup torn fresh basil leaves
1/2 cup thinly sliced red onion
1/3 cup pitted kalamata olives, cut into halves

For the vinaigrette, whisk the vinegar, water, olive oil, garlic, pepper and salt in a small bowl until mixed.

For the salad, cut the bread into 1-inch cubes. Arrange the bread cubes in a single layer on a baking sheet. Spray the cubes with garlic-flavor nonstick cooking spray. Toast at 350 degrees for 15 minutes or until light brown, stirring occasionally. Combine the tomatoes, beans, basil, onion and olives in a large bowl and mix gently. Drizzle with the vinaigrette and toss to coat. Add the toasted bread cubes and mix well. Serve immediately.
Yield: 4 (2-cup) servings.

PER SERVING:
CALORIES: 255; CARBOHYDRATE: 39.9 g; PROTEIN: 9.8 g; TOTAL FAT: 8.1 g;
CHOLESTEROL: 0 mg; SODIUM: 338 mg; FIBER: 8.2 g;
CALORIES FROM FAT: 29%

Your resting metabolic rate (RMR) is the number of calories you burn in one day. If it is high, you may find that you can eat a lot and not gain weight. If your RMR is low, you may eat a low number of calories and be active but still not lose any weight.

RMR depends on gender, age, body composition, and genetics. Muscle burns more calories which is why men generally have a higher RMR than women.

For the most part you cannot change your RMR. Exercise, however, specifically strength training that develops muscle mass, will boost your overall metabolic rate.

APPETIZERS, SOUPS AND SALADS

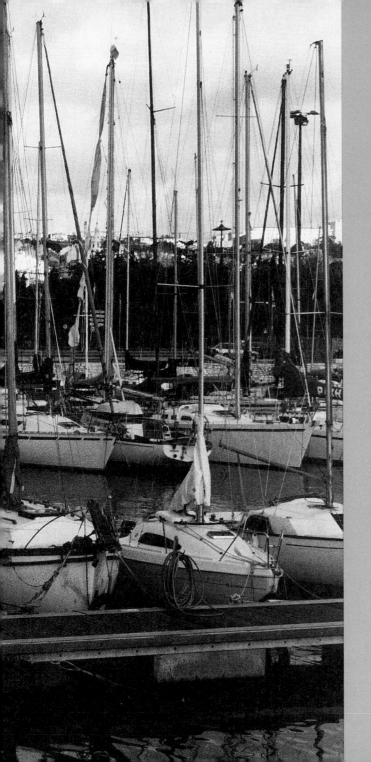

MAIN COURSES

Main courses reflect the Mediterranean Diet Pyramid and a culture that promotes good health.

The mainstay of the diet of this region is grains and pulses, another name for lentils, peas, and beans. Fish, poultry, and small portions of lean meat are also main course staples. Many dishes are combinations, such as stews and tagines, which preserve all the nutrients of the food in a rich broth, and are served over grains such as couscous or rice.

There are distinctive tastes and touches that characterize the Mediterranean style. You can simulate them without fat by using a twist of lemon zest or a splash of lemon juice, a clove of crushed garlic, a sprinkling of mint or herbs, or a dollop of nonfat yogurt every now and then.

From the familiar and beloved dishes of Italy and Greece to the more unusual and distinctive tastes of Morocco, Spain, and countries of the Middle East, the main courses described here are considered part of the art of cooking. Enjoy them the Mediterranean way—at a leisurely pace and in good company.

FOOL
(FUL)

1 (15-ounce) can no-salt-added chick-peas, drained
1 (15-ounce) can fava beans
1/2 cup water
5 garlic cloves
1/8 teaspoon salt
Juice of 2 lemons
1 tablespoon olive oil
1/2 cup chopped tomato
1/4 cup chopped fresh parsley
1/4 cup chopped radishes
1/4 cup chopped green onions

Combine the chick-peas, undrained fava beans and water in a medium saucepan. Bring to a simmer. Simmer for 30 minutes, stirring occasionally. Drain, reserving the liquid. Return the beans to the saucepan. Mash the garlic with the salt using a mortar and pestle. Stir in the lemon juice. Add the garlic mixture to the beans and mix well. Using the pestle coarsely mash the bean mixture, adding enough of the reserved liquid until the bean mixture is the consistency of thin mashed potatoes. Divide the bean mixture evenly among 4 small bowls. Drizzle each serving with 3/4 teaspoon olive oil. Sprinkle evenly with the tomato, parsley, radishes and green onions. Serve with pita bread. Decrease the sodium content of this recipe by substituting dried fava beans or broad beans cooked in water without added salt for the canned fava beans. This will decrease the sodium content to 93 milligrams per serving. **Yield:** 4 (1-cup) servings.

PER SERVING:
CALORIES: 218; CARBOHYDRATE: 32 g; PROTEIN: 12.2 g; TOTAL FAT: 4.9 g;
CHOLESTEROL: 0 mg; SODIUM: 552 mg; FIBER: 9.6 g;
CALORIES FROM FAT: 20%

MAIN COURSES

Fava Bean Cakes with Red Peppers and Yogurt

2 cups canned fava beans, drained and rinsed
1 onion, chopped
1/4 cup egg substitute
3 tablespoons flour
1 tablespoon olive oil
1 tablespoon fresh lemon juice
2 teaspoons minced garlic
1 tablespoon chopped fresh Italian parsley
2 to 3 tablespoons olive oil
1 cup plain fat-free yogurt
1 red bell pepper, chopped (optional)
1 tablespoon chopped fresh Italian parsley

Combine the fava beans, onion, egg substitute, flour, 1 tablespoon olive oil, lemon juice, garlic and 1 tablespoon parsley in a food processor. Process until coarsely chopped and well mixed. Heat 2 to 3 tablespoons olive oil in a large skillet over medium heat. Drop the bean mixture by 1/4 cupfuls into the hot oil and repeat the process until the skillet is full. Cook for 2 to 3 minutes or until firm and light brown; turn. Cook until light brown. Remove the bean cakes to a platter and cover to keep warm. Repeat the process with the remaining bean mixture. Spoon some of the yogurt over each bean cake and sprinkle with the bell pepper and 1 tablespoon parsley. Serve immediately. **Yield:** 4 servings.

PER SERVING:
CALORIES: 219; CARBOHYDRATE: 25 g; PROTEIN: 11 g; TOTAL FAT: 8 g;
CHOLESTEROL: 4 mg; SODIUM: 125 mg; FIBER: 5 g;
CALORIES FROM FAT: 33%

Fava beans, also called broad beans, may be purchased at Middle Eastern markets.

MAIN COURSES

Eggplant, Potato and Chick-Pea Bake

1 large red bell pepper or yellow bell pepper
1 cup fresh basil leaves
1 cup fresh cilantro sprigs
1 tablespoon olive oil
2 garlic cloves
1/4 teaspoon cumin
12 ounces Yukon gold potatoes or red potatoes, thinly sliced
2 cups chopped seeded tomatoes (about 1 pound)
1 (1-pound) eggplant, cut into 2-inch pieces
1 (15-ounce) can chick-peas or garbanzo beans, drained
1 large onion, cut into 8 wedges (about 8 ounces)
1/2 cup water
1/4 teaspoon salt
1/4 teaspoon freshly ground pepper
6 lemon wedges (optional)

Cut the bell pepper lengthwise into halves and discard the seeds and membranes. Arrange the bell pepper halves skin side up on a baking sheet lined with foil; flatten with hand. Broil for 10 minutes or until blackened. Place the bell pepper halves in a sealable plastic bag and seal tightly. Let stand for 10 minutes. Remove the skin and cut into large strips. Combine the basil, cilantro, olive oil, garlic and cumin in a food processor. Process until finely minced. Combine the basil mixture, bell pepper, potatoes, tomatoes, eggplant, chick-peas, onion, water, salt and pepper in a 9×13-inch baking dish and mix well. Bake, covered with foil, at 375 degrees for 1 hour. Remove the foil and stir. Bake for 20 minutes longer or until the vegetables are tender. Serve with lemon wedges.
Yield: 4 (2-cup) servings.

Per Serving:
Calories: 324; Carbohydrate: 58.5 g; Protein: 12.8 g; Total Fat: 6.6 g;
Cholesterol: 0 mg; Sodium: 302 mg; Fiber: 11 g;
Calories from Fat: 18%

Hummus-Stuffed Pitas with Roasted Vegetables

Roasted Vegetables

5 cups (1-inch cubes) peeled eggplant (about 1 pound)
2 cups coarsely chopped red onions
1 1/2 cups coarsely chopped tomatoes
1 cup (1-inch pieces) green bell pepper
2 tablespoons chopped fresh parsley
1 tablespoon chopped fresh thyme, or 1 teaspoon dried thyme
2 teaspoons chopped fresh rosemary, or 1/2 teaspoon dried rosemary
1/4 teaspoon salt ♦ 1/4 teaspoon pepper

Hummus and Assembly

1 (19-ounce) can chick-peas or garbanzo beans, drained
1/4 cup tahini (sesame seed paste)
1/4 cup fresh lemon juice ♦ 2 garlic cloves, chopped
1 tablespoon warm water
1 teaspoon cumin ♦ 1/4 teaspoon pepper
4 (6-inch) whole wheat pita rounds, cut into halves

For the vegetables, toss the eggplant, onions, tomatoes, bell pepper, parsley, thyme, rosemary, salt and pepper in a large shallow roasting pan sprayed with nonstick cooking spray. Roast at 350 degrees for 30 minutes or until the vegetables are tender, stirring occasionally.

For the hummus, combine the chick-peas, tahini, lemon juice, garlic, warm water, cumin and pepper in a food processor. Process until smooth.

To serve, spread the inside of each pita half with 1/4 cup of the hummus and fill each with 1/2 cup of the roasted vegetables.
Yield: 8 (1-pita half) servings.

PER SERVING:
CALORIES: 261; CARBOHYDRATE: 43.8 g; PROTEIN: 10.5 g; TOTAL FAT: 6.8 g;
CHOLESTEROL: 0 mg; SODIUM: 364 mg; FIBER: 7.9 g;
CALORIES FROM FAT: 23%

Main Courses

LENTIL CASSEROLE

3/4 cup dried lentils
3/4 cup brown rice
1/2 cup chopped onion
1/4 cup shredded low-fat sharp Cheddar cheese
1/2 teaspoon thyme
1/2 teaspoon basil
1/2 teaspoon oregano
1/4 teaspoon garlic powder
1/8 teaspoon sage
1/4 cup water
4 cups defatted reduced-sodium chicken broth,
vegetable broth or apple juice

Sort and rinse the lentils. Combine the lentils, brown rice, onion, cheese, thyme, basil, oregano, garlic power, sage and water in a bowl and mix well. Stir in the broth. Pour the lentil mixture into a 1 1/2-quart baking dish sprayed with nonstick cooking spray. Bake, covered, at 350 degrees for 1 1/2 hours or until the lentils are tender. **Yield:** 6 (1-cup) servings.

PER SERVING:
CALORIES: 154; CARBOHYDRATE: 27.4 g; PROTEIN: 10.3 g; TOTAL FAT: 2.2 g;
CHOLESTEROL: 1.6 mg; SODIUM: 73 mg; FIBER: 5.1 g;
CALORIES FROM FAT: 13%

MAIN COURSES

Brown Lentils and Rice with Caramelized Onions
(Megadarra)

3 tablespoons extra-virgin olive oil
7 cups vertically sliced onions
4 1/2 cups water
1 1/4 cups dried brown lentils, sorted and rinsed
1 1/4 cups long grain rice
1 teaspoon salt
1/4 teaspoon pepper
1 tablespoon extra-virgin olive oil

Heat 3 tablespoons olive oil in a large skillet over medium-low heat. Stir in the onions. Cook, covered, for 15 minutes or until tender, stirring occasionally; remove the cover. Increase the heat to medium. Cook for 25 minutes longer or until golden brown, stirring occasionally. Remove from the heat and cover to keep warm. Bring the water to a boil in a large saucepan. Stir in the lentils. Cook for 20 minutes or until tender, stirring occasionally. Reserve 1/2 cup of the caramelized onions. Add the remaining caramelized onions, rice, salt and pepper to the lentils and mix well. Cook, covered, for 25 minutes or until the lentils and rice are tender. Spoon the lentil mixture into a shallow serving dish. Top with the reserved caramelized onions and drizzle with 1 tablespoon olive oil.
Yield: 11 (1/2-cup) servings.

Per Serving:
Calories: 222; Carbohydrate: 35.6 g; Protein: 8.5 g; Total Fat: 5.4 g;
Cholesterol: 0 mg; Sodium: 222 mg; Fiber: 8.3 g;
Calories from Fat: 22%

Megadarra (me-ga-DAR-ra) is immensely popular in the Middle East. It is served either warm or at room temperature as a meze or appetizer, and is often accompanied by yogurt.

Main Courses

Pasta with Spinach, Artichokes, Portobellos and Gorgonzola

8 ounces pasta, such as capellini or fusilli
2 tablespoons olive oil
8 ounces sliced portobello mushrooms
2 teaspoons minced garlic
1 bunch fresh spinach or broccoli rabe, trimmed
2 tablespoons balsamic vinegar
2 ounces Gorgonzola cheese, crumbled
1 cup water-pack artichoke heart quarters
Crushed red pepper to taste

Bring a saucepan of water to a boil over high heat. Add the pasta and stir. Cook for 5 to 7 minutes or until al dente. Drain the pasta and place in a colander. Rinse with cold water. Heat the olive oil in a large skillet over medium heat. Sauté the mushrooms and garlic in the hot oil for 2 to 3 minutes; turn the mushroom slices. Sauté until tender. Slice the spinach crosswise into 1-inch strips. Add half the spinach to the mushroom mixture. Cook until the spinach wilts, stirring constantly. Stir in the remaining spinach and vinegar. Cook until the spinach wilts, stirring constantly. Add the pasta, cheese and artichokes. Cook until the cheese melts, stirring constantly. Remove from the heat. Season with red pepper. Serve immediately. **Yield:** 4 servings.

Per Serving:
Calories: 398; Carbohydrate: 56 g; Protein: 15 g; Total Fat: 14 g;
Cholesterol: 19 mg; Sodium: 262 mg; Fiber: 4 g;
Calories from Fat: 32%

Tomato Basil Pizza

2 teaspoons olive oil
1/8 teaspoon salt
1/8 teaspoon pepper
1/4 cup thinly sliced fresh basil
2 tablespoons chopped fresh oregano
2 (10-inch) Quick and Easy Pizza Crusts (page 147)
4 plum tomatoes, thinly sliced (about 8 ounces)
1 cup (4 ounces) shredded part-skim mozzarella cheese

Mix the olive oil, salt and pepper in a small bowl. Toss the basil and oregano in a small bowl. Brush each pizza crust with 1/2 of the olive oil mixture and top each with 1/2 of the tomatoes, 1/2 of the cheese and 1/2 of the basil mixture. Bake at 425 degrees for 10 minutes or until the cheese melts and the crust is light brown. **Yield:** 6 (1/3-pizza) servings.

Per Serving:
Calories: 286; Carbohydrate: 41.6 g; Protein: 11.7 g; Total Fat: 8.3 g; Cholesterol: 11 mg; Sodium: 289 mg; Fiber: 1.8 g; Calories from Fat: 26%

Main Courses

An easy way to determine a
healthy weight is by
using the Body Mass Index
(BMI). This is a simple
calculation that compares
your height to your weight.
A BMI chart is located on
page 9 in this book.

For men, desirable
BMI is 22 to 24.
Above 28.5 is overweight,
and a BMI above 33 is
seriously overweight.

For women, desirable BMI
is 21 to 23. Above 27.5
is considered overweight,
and a BMI above 31.5
is seriously overweight.

MAIN COURSES

SPINACH AND CHEESE PIE

Crust
4 cups cooked brown rice, barley or bulgur
1/4 cup egg substitute, or 2 egg whites, lightly beaten

Spinach Filling
2 (10-ounce) packages frozen chopped spinach, thawed and drained
2 cups sliced fresh mushrooms
2 tablespoons dry white wine or water
2 cups evaporated skim milk
2 cups egg substitute
2 cups (8 ounces) shredded nonfat or reduced-fat mozzarella cheese
1/4 cup minced fresh parsley
1 teaspoon crushed garlic
1 teaspoon thyme
1/4 teaspoon pepper
1/4 cup (1 ounce) grated nonfat or reduced-fat Parmesan cheese

For the crust, combine the brown rice and egg substitute in a medium bowl and mix well. Pat the rice mixture with the back of a spoon over the bottoms and up the sides of 2 deep-dish 9-inch pie plates sprayed with nonstick cooking spray.

For the filling, press the excess moisture from the spinach. Combine the mushrooms and wine in a 3-quart saucepan. Cook over medium heat until the mushrooms are tender and the liquid has evaporated, stirring constantly. Remove from the heat. Stir in the spinach, evaporated skim milk, egg substitute, mozzarella cheese, parsley, garlic, thyme and pepper in the order listed, stirring well after each addition. Spoon 1/2 of the filling into each prepared pie plate. Sprinkle each with 2 tablespoons of the Parmesan cheese. Bake at 375 degrees for 45 minutes or until a sharp knife inserted in the center comes out clean. Let stand for 5 minutes before serving. **Yield:** 10 servings.

PER SERVING:
CALORIES: 198; CARBOHYDRATE: 26.7 g; PROTEIN: 20.5 g; TOTAL FAT: 0.8 g;
CHOLESTEROL: 7 mg; SODIUM: 340 mg; FIBER: 2.5 g;
CALORIES FROM FAT: 4%

Lemon Oregano Grouper with Vegetables

2 small zucchini, julienned
1 cup fresh or frozen whole kernel corn
1/4 cup chopped red bell pepper
1 tablespoon olive oil
1/4 teaspoon salt
4 (5-ounce) grouper fillets, 1 inch thick
1/8 teaspoon salt
Freshly ground pepper to taste
2 tablespoons coarsely chopped fresh oregano
1 tablespoon olive oil
2 teaspoons lemon juice
4 paper-thin slices lemon, cut into halves

Toss the zucchini, corn, bell pepper, 1 tablespoon olive oil and 1/4 teaspoon salt in a bowl until coated. Mound 1/4 of the vegetable mixture in the center of each of 4 large sheets of foil. Sprinkle the fillets with 1/8 teaspoon salt and pepper. Arrange 1 fillet over each mound of vegetables. Combine the oregano, 1 tablespoon olive oil and lemon juice in a small bowl and mix well. Drizzle 1/4 of the oregano mixture over each fillet and top each with 2 lemon halves. Seal the packet by rolling up the top and sides. Bake at 375 degrees for 16 to 20 minutes or until the fillets flake easily when tested with a fork. Place each packet on a serving plate and open carefully to allow the steam to escape.
Yield: 4 (1 fillet with vegetables) servings.

Per Serving:
Calories: 239; Carbohydrate: 10 g; Protein: 30.4 g; Total Fat: 9 g;
Cholesterol: 52 mg; Sodium: 102 mg; Fiber: 1.8 g;
Calories from Fat: 33%

Main Courses

TURKISH FISH SANDWICHES

4 (6-ounce) grouper fillets, 3/4 inch thick
2 teaspoons olive oil
1/8 teaspoon salt
1/2 teaspoon freshly ground pepper
1 (6-ounce) French baguette
1/4 cup Muhammara (page 63)
1 teaspoon fresh lemon juice
1 cup thinly sliced onion
1 cup thinly sliced poblano chiles
1 cup chopped tomato

Brush both sides of the fillets with the olive oil and sprinkle with the salt and pepper. Arrange the fillets on a grill rack sprayed with nonstick cooking spray. Grill over hot coals for 5 minutes per side or until the fillets flake easily when tested with a fork. Cut the bread into four 1 1/2-ounce slices and cut each slice horizontally into halves. Spread 1 tablespoon of the Muhammara over the top halves of the bread slices. Arrange the fillets on the bottom halves. Sprinkle each fillet with 1/4 teaspoon of the lemon juice and top with 1/4 cup of the onion, 1/4 cup of the poblano chiles and 1/4 cup of the tomato. Top with the remaining bread halves. Serve immediately. **Yield:** 4 servings.

PER SERVING:
CALORIES: 336; CARBOHYDRATE: 35.8 g; PROTEIN: 31.2 g; TOTAL FAT: 7.5 g;
CHOLESTEROL: 47 mg; SODIUM: 544 mg; FIBER: 3.7 g;
CALORIES FROM FAT: 20%

MAIN COURSES

Red Snapper with Cilantro Lime Vinaigrette

1/4 cup olive oil
2 tablespoons lime juice
2 tablespoons sugar
2 tablespoons red wine vinegar
1 shallot, finely chopped (optional)
1 tablespoon snipped fresh cilantro
1 garlic clove, minced
1/2 teaspoon lime zest
1 lime, cut into 4 wedges
4 (6-ounce) red snapper fillets or other firm white fish fillets,
skinned (1 inch thick)

Combine the olive oil, lime juice, sugar, vinegar, shallot, cilantro, garlic and lime zest in a bowl and mix well. Reserve 2 tablespoons of the oil mixture. Arrange the fillets in a single layer in a shallow dish. Drizzle with the remaining oil mixture. Marinate, covered, in the refrigerator for 30 to 60 minutes, turning occasionally. Drain, reserving the marinade. Arrange the fillets on a greased broiler rack in a broiler pan. Broil 4 inches from the heat source for 8 to 12 minutes or until the fillets flake easily when tested with a fork, turning once and brushing with the reserved marinade halfway through the broiling process; discard the remaining marinade. Arrange 1 fillet on each of 4 serving plates. Drizzle with the reserved oil mixture. Serve immediately with the lime wedges. **Yield:** 4 servings.

Per Serving:
Calories: 249; Carbohydrate: 6 g; Protein: 35 g; Total Fat: 9 g;
Cholesterol: 62 mg; Sodium: 110 mg; Fiber: 1 g;
Calories from Fat: 32%
Nutritional information includes the entire amount of the marinade.

Main Courses

Serve Garlic Spinach Topping over grilled or baked salmon fillets or steaks. Sauté ½ cup finely chopped onion and 3 minced large garlic cloves in a large nonstick skillet sprayed with nonstick cooking spray for 3 minutes. Stir in 2 tablespoons malt vinegar. Cook for 30 seconds or until the liquid evaporates, stirring constantly. Add ⅓ cup water. Cook for 4 minutes or until the mixture is reduced by ½. Stir in 8 cups firmly packed torn fresh spinach, ¼ teaspoon salt and ⅛ teaspoon pepper. Cook for 3 minutes or until the spinach wilts, stirring constantly. Spoon over grilled or baked salmon fillets.

MAIN COURSES

✓

BAKED FISH WITH GARLIC AND CILANTRO

4 (4-ounce) fresh fish fillets, such as salmon, red snapper, grouper or orange roughy
2 garlic cloves
⅛ teaspoon salt
¼ cup chopped fresh cilantro
3 tablespoons lemon juice
1 tablespoon olive oil
¼ teaspoon black pepper
⅛ teaspoon cumin
⅛ teaspoon red pepper
1 lemon, sliced
Sprigs of fresh parsley (optional)

Arrange the fillets in a single layer in a shallow baking dish sprayed with nonstick cooking spray. Crush the garlic with the salt in a bowl until of a paste consistency. Add the cilantro, lemon juice, olive oil, black pepper, cumin and red pepper to the garlic mixture and mix well. Spread the garlic mixture over the top of the fillets and top with the lemon slices. Bake at 350 degrees for 15 to 30 minutes or until the fillets flake easily when tested with a fork. The cooking time will vary according to the thickness of the fillets. Garnish each serving with sprigs of parsley. **Yield:** 4 servings.

PER SERVING:
CALORIES: 153; CARBOHYDRATE: 2.9 g; PROTEIN: 23.4 g; TOTAL FAT: 5 g;
CHOLESTEROL: 41 mg; SODIUM: 144 mg; FIBER: 0.5 g;
CALORIES FROM FAT: 29%

Baked Fish Mediterranean Style

12 large fresh basil leaves, or 1 teaspoon dried basil
4 (5-ounce) fish fillets, such as red snapper, grouper or orange roughy
1/8 teaspoon salt
3 large garlic cloves, finely minced
4 teaspoons drained capers
8 Greek olives, sliced
2 plum tomatoes, each cut into 8 thin slices
1 lemon, cut into halves
4 sprigs of fresh rosemary, or 1/4 teaspoon dried rosemary
Freshly ground pepper to taste

Layer the basil leaves over the bottom of a baking dish sprayed with nonstick cooking spray. Arrange the fillets in a single layer over the basil and sprinkle with the salt. Top each fillet with 1/4 of the garlic, 1 teaspoon of the capers, 1/4 of the olives and 4 tomato slices. Cut 1 of the lemon halves into 4 slices. Squeeze the juice from the remaining lemon half evenly over the fillets. Top each fillet with 1 lemon slice and 1 sprig of the rosemary. Sprinkle with pepper. Bake, covered, at 425 degrees for 15 to 20 minutes or until the fillets flake easily when tested with a fork. The cooking time will vary according to the thickness of the fillets. **Yield:** 4 servings.

Per Serving:
Calories: 150; Carbohydrate: 2.9 g; Protein: 28 g; Total Fat: 2.4 g;
Cholesterol: 52 mg; Sodium: 273 mg; Fiber: 0.6 g;
Calories from Fat: 14%

Main Courses

MAIN COURSES

Moroccan Sea Bass

Spice Rub
2 tablespoons coriander
2 teaspoons freshly ground pepper
1 teaspoon caraway seeds
1 teaspoon cumin ♦ 1 teaspoon paprika
¹/4 teaspoon salt

Marinade
¹/4 cup fresh lemon juice ♦ 3 garlic cloves, crushed
1 tablespoon minced fresh cilantro
1 teaspoon cumin
¹/4 teaspoon crushed red pepper

Sea Bass
4 (6-ounce) sea bass fillets, 1 inch thick
1 tablespoon olive oil ♦ Lemon wedges (optional)
Sprigs of fresh cilantro (optional)

For the rub, mix the coriander, pepper, caraway seeds, cumin, paprika and salt in a small bowl.

For the marinade, combine the lemon juice, garlic, cilantro, cumin and red pepper in a sealable plastic bag.

For the sea bass, add the fillets to the sealable plastic bag and seal tightly. Turn to coat. Marinate in the refrigerator for 45 minutes, turning occasionally. Drain, discarding the marinade. Coat the fillets with the rub. Heat the olive oil in a large nonstick skillet over medium heat. Cook the fillets in the hot oil for 6 minutes per side or until the fillets flake easily when tested with a fork. Garnish each serving with lemon wedges and sprigs of fresh cilantro. **Yield:** 4 servings.

PER SERVING:
CALORIES: 210; CARBOHYDRATE: 3.2 g; PROTEIN: 32.1 g; TOTAL FAT: 7.2 g; CHOLESTEROL: 70 mg; SODIUM: 267 mg; FIBER: 0.7 g; CALORIES FROM FAT: 30%
Nutritional information includes the entire amount of the marinade.

SWORDFISH KABOBS

Marinade
1 cup chopped onion
Juice of 2 lemons
2 tablespoons olive oil
4 large garlic cloves, minced
1 teaspoon cumin
1 teaspoon paprika
1/2 teaspoon black peppercorns
1/4 teaspoon crushed red pepper
1/4 teaspoon salt

Swordfish
1 pound swordfish, cut into 1/2-inch cubes
1 pint large cherry tomatoes
4 poblano chiles, seeded and cut into 1-inch pieces

For the marinade, combine the onion, lemon juice, olive oil, garlic, cumin, paprika, black peppercorns, red pepper and salt in a food processor. Process until smooth.

For the swordfish, combine the marinade and swordfish in a bowl and mix gently. Marinate, covered, in the refrigerator for 30 minutes, stirring occasionally. Remove the swordfish to a platter, reserving the marinade. Thread the swordfish, tomatoes and poblano chiles evenly on eight 12-inch skewers. Arrange the kabobs on a grill rack coated with nonstick cooking spray. Grill over hot coals for 10 minutes or until the swordfish flakes easily when tested with a fork, turning and basting with the reserved marinade frequently. **Yield:** 4 (2-kabob) servings.

PER SERVING:
CALORIES: 245; CARBOHYDRATE: 20.3 g; PROTEIN: 25.4 g; TOTAL FAT: 7.7 g;
CHOLESTEROL: 44 mg; SODIUM: 271 mg; FIBER: 5.1 g;
CALORIES FROM FAT: 28%
Nutritional information includes the entire amount of the marinade.

Swordfish kabobs are available on the streets of Istanbul, where they are often served wrapped in a warm pide (flatbread). They can also be served with rice pilaf.

MAIN COURSES

SCALLOPS AND ASPARAGUS WITH ANGEL HAIR PASTA

1/3 pound fresh asparagus spears
4 ounces angel hair pasta
2 teaspoons grated lemon zest
2 teaspoons fresh lemon juice
2 teaspoons olive oil
1 teaspoon dill weed
1 1/2 teaspoons grated Parmesan cheese (made with skim milk)
8 ounces bay scallops, rinsed and drained
2 garlic cloves, minced
1/2 cup clam juice
1 1/2 teaspoons grated Parmesan cheese (made with skim milk)
2 lemon wedges
Sprigs of fresh dill weed (optional)

Snap off the woody ends of the asparagus spears and discard. Place the asparagus in a microwave-safe dish. Microwave, covered, on High for 2 minutes. Submerge the asparagus in cold water immediately; drain. Cut the spears into 2-inch pieces. Cook the pasta in a saucepan using package directions without added fat or salt; drain. Return the pasta to the saucepan. Stir in the lemon zest, lemon juice, olive oil, dill weed and 1 1/2 teaspoons cheese. Cover to keep warm.

Heat a medium nonstick skillet sprayed with butter-flavor nonstick cooking spray over medium-high heat. Add the scallops and garlic to the hot skillet. Sauté until the scallops are brown and tender. Add the asparagus and clam juice and mix well. Cook for 2 minutes, stirring frequently. Arrange 1/2 of the pasta on each of 2 serving plates. Top each serving with 1/2 of the scallop mixture. Sprinkle with 1 1/2 teaspoons cheese. Garnish with the lemon wedges and sprigs of dill weed. **Yield:** 2 servings.

PER SERVING:
CALORIES: 386; CARBOHYDRATE: 49 g; PROTEIN: 30.7 g; TOTAL FAT: 7 g;
CHOLESTEROL: 44.2 mg; SODIUM: 328 mg; FIBER: 2.4 g;
CALORIES FROM FAT: 16%

MAIN COURSES

Pesto Shrimp

2 tablespoons chopped fresh parsley
Juice of 1 lemon
3 garlic cloves, minced
1 tablespoon chopped fresh oregano
1 tablespoon chopped fresh basil
1 teaspoon olive oil
Pepper to taste
1¹/₂ pounds large shrimp, peeled and deveined

Combine the parsley, lemon juice, garlic, oregano, basil, olive oil and pepper in a bowl and mix well. Add the shrimp and toss to coat. Marinate, covered, in the refrigerator for 8 to 10 hours, stirring occasionally. Heat a skillet sprayed with nonstick cooking spray over medium-high heat. Sauté the shrimp mixture in the hot skillet for 4 minutes or until the shrimp turn pink. **Yield:** 6 (3.5-ounce) servings.

PER SERVING:
CALORIES: 132; CARBOHYDRATE: 2.5 g; PROTEIN: 23.3 g; TOTAL FAT: 2.8 g;
CHOLESTEROL: 172 mg; SODIUM: 169 mg; FIBER: 0.3 g;
CALORIES FROM FAT: 19%

Cardiorespiratory Endurance is the ability of the heart and blood vessels to sustain physical activity for long periods of time. A fit person has a lower resting heart and greater stroke volume (heart pumping ability) versus an unfit person.

Muscle Strength refers to the maximum amount of weight a person can lift one time.

Muscle Endurance is the ability to perform repeated muscular contractions such as doing multiple sit-ups, pull-ups, or push-ups.

Flexibility is the ability of your joints to move freely through a full range of motion.

MAIN COURSES

CHICKEN CACCIATORE WITH FETTUCCINI

8 ounces boneless skinless chicken breasts
2 tablespoons flour
1 cup sliced onion
2 teaspoons olive oil
2 cups canned chopped no-salt-added tomatoes
1 cup sliced carrots
2 teaspoons oregano
2 cups hot cooked fettuccini

Coat the chicken with the flour. Sauté the chicken and onion in the olive oil in a large nonstick skillet. Stir in the tomatoes, carrots and oregano. Cook, covered, for 20 minutes or until the chicken is cooked through, stirring occasionally. Serve over the hot cooked pasta.
Yield: 2 servings.

PER SERVING:
CALORIES: 487; CARBOHYDRATE: 63 g; PROTEIN: 35 g; TOTAL FAT: 8.6 g;
CHOLESTEROL: 73 mg; SODIUM: 148 mg; FIBER: 8 g;
CALORIES FROM FAT: 16%

MAIN COURSES

Chicken in Garlic Sauce

2 chicken breasts, skinned
2 chicken drumsticks, skinned
2 chicken thighs, skinned
1/4 teaspoon salt
1 tablespoon olive oil
10 garlic cloves, crushed
1 dried hot red chile
1/4 cup fat-free less-sodium chicken broth
2 tablespoons dry white wine
1/4 teaspoon saffron powder or turmeric
1 bay leaf
2 tablespoons minced fresh parsley

Sprinkle the chicken with the salt. Heat the olive oil in a large nonstick skillet over medium-high heat. Arrange the chicken in the hot skillet. Cook for 5 minutes or until golden brown; turn the chicken. Add the garlic and red chile to the hot skillet and mix well. Stir in the broth, wine, saffron and bay leaf. Bring to a boil; reduce the heat. Simmer, covered, for 30 minutes or until the chicken is cooked through, stirring occasionally. Discard the red chile and bay leaf. Sprinkle each serving with the parsley.
Yield: 4 (3 ounces chicken and 3 tablespoons sauce) servings.

Per Serving:
Calories: 238; Carbohydrate: 3 g; Protein: 37 g; Total Fat: 7.8 g;
Cholesterol: 120 mg; Sodium: 253 mg; Fiber: 0.2 g;
Calories from Fat: 30%

Coat cuts of lamb, beef, chicken or pork with Thyme, Rosemary and Chive Herb Crust. Mix 1/2 teaspoon finely chopped garlic (optional), 2 teaspoons each coarsely chopped fresh rosemary and thyme, 2 teaspoons each finely chopped fresh parsley and chives, 1 teaspoon lemon zest, 1 teaspoon coarsely ground pepper and 1/2 teaspoon ground sea salt in a bowl. Cover the bottom of a dish with the herb mixture. Lightly brush the desired cut of meat with 1 tablespoon olive oil and then generously coat all sides with the herb mixture. Roast, sear or grill as desired.

Main Courses

Chicken with Chick-Peas or Ferakh bel Hummus (pronounced fi-ra-KAH bel hoo-Mus) can be served with plain rice. The combination of spices, garlic, and lemon yields a special flavor characteristic of the area. Chick-peas are used in many dishes in the Middle East.

CHICKEN WITH CHICK-PEAS
(FERAKH BEL HUMMUS)

1 tablespoon olive oil
1 cup finely chopped onion
1/2 teaspoon turmeric
4 chicken breasts, skinned
2 1/2 cups water
2 tablespoons fresh lemon juice
1/2 teaspoon salt
1/4 teaspoon pepper
3 garlic cloves, crushed
2 (15-ounce) cans no-salt-added chick-peas or
garbanzo beans, drained

Heat the olive oil in a large Dutch oven over medium heat. Cook the onion in the hot oil for 12 minutes or until golden brown, stirring frequently. Stir in the turmeric. Add the chicken to the onion mixture and turn to coat. Stir in the water, lemon juice, salt, pepper and garlic. Bring to a boil; reduce the heat. Simmer, covered, for 1 hour or until the chicken is tender, stirring occasionally. Remove from the heat. Using a slotted spoon, remove the chicken to a platter. Cut the chicken into bite-size pieces, discarding the bones. Return the chicken to the Dutch oven. Stir in the chick-peas. Cook for 5 minutes or until heated through, stirring frequently. **Yield:** 6 (1-cup) servings.

PER SERVING:
CALORIES: 256; CARBOHYDRATE: 23.3 g; PROTEIN: 26.5 g; TOTAL FAT: 6 g;
CHOLESTEROL: 73 mg; SODIUM: 184 mg; FIBER: 6.3 g;
CALORIES FROM FAT: 21%

MAIN COURSES

CHICKEN PICCATA

✓

4 boneless skinless chicken breasts
1/3 cup flour
1 tablespoon olive oil
1/2 cup chopped onion
2 garlic cloves, minced
1/2 teaspoon chicken bouillon granules
1/2 cup hot water
Juice of 1/2 lemon
1/2 lemon, sliced (optional)
4 sprigs of fresh parsley (optional)

Pound the chicken 1/4 inch thick between sheets of waxed paper with a meat mallet. Coat the chicken with the flour. Spray a 10-inch sauté pan generously with nonstick cooking spray and add the olive oil. Sauté the chicken in the olive oil over medium heat for 2 1/2 minutes per side. Remove the chicken to paper towels to drain, reserving the pan drippings. Sauté the onion and garlic in the reserved pan drippings for 1 to 2 minutes. Drain the onion mixture on a paper towel. Wipe the excess oil from the sauté pan. Return the chicken and onion mixture to the sauté pan. Dissolve the bouillon in the hot water in a cup and pour over the chicken. Drizzle with the lemon juice. Simmer, covered, for 5 minutes or until the chicken is cooked through. Arrange the chicken on a serving platter. Garnish with the lemon slices and sprigs of parsley. **Yield:** 4 servings.

PER SERVING:
CALORIES: 221; CARBOHYDRATE: 12 g; PROTEIN: 28 g; TOTAL FAT: 6.5 g;
CHOLESTEROL: 73 mg; SODIUM: 212 mg; FIBER: 0.5 g;
CALORIES FROM FAT: 26%

MAIN COURSES

To toast nuts on top of the stove: Place the nuts in a dry nonstick skillet over medium-high heat. Shake the pan back and forth, or stir with a wooden spoon for 2 to 3 minutes, watching carefully until the nuts turn a light brown. Remove the nuts from the pan. Let stand until cool.

To toast in the oven: Preheat the oven to 375 degrees. Spread the nuts in a single layer on a baking sheet. Bake for 5 to 8 minutes or until light brown, stirring once or twice.

Main Courses

Artichoke-Stuffed Chicken Breasts

1/2 cup (2 ounces) crumbled feta cheese
1/4 cup drained water-pack artichoke hearts, finely chopped
1 roasted red bell pepper, chopped
2 tablespoons chopped fresh basil
2 tablespoons pine nuts, toasted
2 teaspoons red wine vinegar
2 garlic cloves, minced
1 teaspoon extra-virgin olive oil
4 (5-ounce) boneless skinless chicken breasts
1/8 teaspoon salt
Freshly ground pepper to taste
1 teaspoon extra-virgin olive oil

Combine the cheese, artichokes, roasted bell pepper, basil, pine nuts, vinegar and garlic in a bowl and mix well. Stir in 1 teaspoon olive oil. Using a thin sharp knife such as a boning knife, make a 2-inch horizontal slit in the thickest part of each chicken breast cutting to but not through the opposite side of the breast. Hold the knife blade parallel to the cutting board and guide the blade around the inside of the breast to create a pocket. Stuff 1/4 cup of the artichoke mixture into each pocket. Sprinkle the chicken with the salt and pepper. Heat 1 teaspoon olive oil in a large nonstick skillet sprayed with nonstick cooking spray. Add the chicken to the hot oil. Cook for 5 to 6 minutes per side or until the chicken is cooked through. **Yield:** 4 servings.

Per Serving:
Calories: 235; Carbohydrate: 4.5 g; Protein: 31 g; Total Fat: 9.6 g;
Cholesterol: 82 mg; Sodium: 211 mg; Fiber: 0.8 g;
Calories from Fat: 36%

Mediterranean Chicken and Vegetable Kabobs

1¹/2 pounds boneless skinless chicken breasts, cut into 24 strips
18 (¹/2-inch-thick) slices zucchini
1 fennel bulb, cut into 12 wedges
¹/4 cup fresh lemon juice
2 tablespoons chopped fresh oregano, or
2 teaspoons dried oregano
2 tablespoons olive oil
12 garlic cloves
¹/2 teaspoon salt
¹/4 teaspoon pepper

Combine the chicken, zucchini, fennel, lemon juice, oregano and olive oil in a sealable plastic bag and seal tightly. Shake to coat. Marinate in the refrigerator for 20 minutes, turning several times. Drain, discarding the marinade. Combine the garlic with enough water to cover in a saucepan. Bring to a boil. Boil for 3 minutes; drain. Let stand until cool. Thread 4 chicken strips, 3 zucchini slices, 2 fennel wedges and 2 garlic cloves alternately on each of six 12-inch skewers. Sprinkle with the salt and pepper. Arrange the skewers on a grill rack sprayed with nonstick cooking spray. Grill over hot coals for 8 minutes or until the chicken is cooked through, turning once. **Yield:** 6 servings.

Per Serving:
Calories: 194; Carbohydrate: 6.4 g; Protein: 28 g; Total Fat: 6.2 g;
Cholesterol: 66 mg; Sodium: 274 mg; Fiber: 0.7 g;
Calories from Fat: 29%
Nutritional information includes the entire amount of the marinade.

Main Courses

Moroccan-Style Chicken

2 teaspoons cumin
1 teaspoon cardamom
1/2 teaspoon cinnamon
1/4 teaspoon red pepper
1/4 teaspoon black pepper
1/8 teaspoon salt
4 boneless skinless chicken breasts
1 tablespoon olive oil
1 (15-ounce) can chick-peas or garbanzo beans, drained
1 (14-ounce) can diced no-salt-added tomatoes, drained
2 cups (1/4-inch-thick) slices zucchini
1/2 cup fat-free less-sodium chicken broth
1 tablespoon fresh lemon juice
Sprigs of fresh cilantro (optional)

Mix the cumin, cardamom, cinnamon, red pepper, black pepper and salt in a bowl. Coat the chicken with the cumin mixture. Heat the olive oil in a large nonstick skillet over medium-high heat. Sauté the chicken in the hot oil for 5 minutes per side. Add the chick-peas and tomatoes to the skillet and mix well. Cook for 5 minutes, stirring frequently. Stir in the zucchini and broth; reduce the heat. Simmer, covered, for 10 minutes, stirring occasionally. Stir in the lemon juice. Garnish with sprigs of cilantro. **Yield:** 4 (1 chicken breast and 1/2 cup chick-pea mixture) servings.

Per Serving:
Calories: 262; Carbohydrate: 25.9 g; Protein: 34.9 g; Total Fat: 7.9 g;
Cholesterol: 73 mg; Sodium: 409 mg; Fiber: 3.1 g;
Calories from Fat: 27%

Main Courses

Chicken with Tomatoes and Artichokes

1 teaspoon olive oil
4 (4-ounce) boneless skinless chicken breasts
1 (14-ounce) can no-salt-added diced tomatoes
1 (14-ounce) can artichoke hearts, drained and rinsed
1 small onion, sliced
4 garlic cloves, minced
1 teaspoon oregano
1/2 teaspoon pepper

Coat a large nonstick skillet with nonstick cooking spray. Add the olive oil to the prepared skillet and heat over medium-high heat. Cook the chicken in the hot oil until brown on both sides, turning once. Add the undrained tomatoes, artichokes, onion, garlic, oregano and pepper and mix well. Cook, covered, for 20 to 25 minutes or until the chicken is cooked through, stirring occasionally. Serve with hot cooked brown rice.
Yield: 4 servings.

Per Serving:
Calories: 196; Carbohydrate: 9.5 g; Protein: 29.7 g; Total Fat: 4.3 g;
Cholesterol: 73 mg; Sodium: 408 mg; Fiber: 4 g;
Calories from Fat: 20%

Main Courses

ITALIAN CHICKEN WITH CHICK-PEAS

1 pound chicken breast tenders
1/4 teaspoon pepper
1 tablespoon olive oil
1 1/3 cups sliced onions
1 cup green bell pepper strips
1 (15-ounce) can no-salt-added chick-peas, drained
1 (14-ounce) can diced tomatoes with basil, garlic and oregano
1 teaspoon minced garlic, or 3 garlic cloves, minced
Fresh flat-leaf parsley leaves (optional)

Sprinkle the chicken with the pepper. Heat the olive oil in a large nonstick skillet over medium-high heat. Cook the chicken in the hot oil for 2 minutes per side or until light brown, stirring frequently. Add the onions and bell pepper to the skillet and mix well. Sauté for 4 minutes. Reduce the heat to medium. Stir in the chick-peas, undrained tomatoes and garlic. Cook, covered, for 8 minutes or until heated through, stirring occasionally. Garnish with parsley leaves. **Yield:** 4 (1 1/2-cup) servings.

PER SERVING:
CALORIES: 296; CARBOHYDRATE: 28.2 g; PROTEIN: 32 g; TOTAL FAT: 6.1 g;
CHOLESTEROL: 66 mg; SODIUM: 257 mg; FIBER: 5.6 g;
CALORIES FROM FAT: 19%

MAIN COURSES

Spicy Pork Kabobs
(Pinchos Morunos)

1/4 cup chopped fresh parsley
2 garlic cloves, minced
1 tablespoon paprika
1 tablespoon olive oil
1 teaspoon oregano
1 teaspoon cumin
1 teaspoon coriander
1/2 teaspoon salt
1/4 teaspoon saffron threads, crushed, or 1/4 teaspoon turmeric
1/4 teaspoon red pepper
1 (1-pound) pork tenderloin, trimmed and cut into 18 cubes
2 small red onions, each cut into 6 wedges
2 red bell peppers, each cut into 6 wedges
2 yellow bell peppers, each cut into 6 wedges

Combine the parsley, garlic, paprika, olive oil, oregano, cumin, coriander, salt, saffron and red pepper in a large bowl and mix well. Add the pork to the garlic mixture and toss to coat. Thread 3 pork cubes, 2 onion wedges, 2 red bell pepper wedges and 2 yellow bell pepper wedges alternately on each of six 12-inch skewers. Arrange the skewers on a grill rack sprayed with nonstick cooking spray. Grill over hot coals for 6 minutes per side or until the pork is cooked through. **Yield:** 6 servings.

Per Serving:
Calories: 143; Carbohydrate: 8.2 g; Protein: 17.2 g; Total Fat: 4.7 g;
Cholesterol: 49 mg; Sodium: 240 mg; Fiber: 4.7 g;
Calories from Fat: 30%

Spicy Pork Kabobs are commonly found in the tapas bars of Spain. Double the serving size for an entrée, or serve as an appetizer.

Main Courses

√

Pan-Roasted Pork Loin with Leeks
(Lombo di Maiale col Porri)

4 large leeks (about 2¹/4 pounds)
¹/2 cup water
¹/8 teaspoon salt
¹/4 teaspoon pepper
2 teaspoons olive oil
1 (2-pound) boneless pork loin, trimmed
¹/2 cup dry white wine
¹/8 teaspoon salt
¹/4 teaspoon pepper
Chopped fresh parsley (optional)

Discard the roots and tough upper leaves from the leeks. Cut each leek lengthwise into halves. Cut each half crosswise into ¹/2-inch slices (about 6 cups). Soak the leek slices in cold water in a bowl to loosen the dirt; drain. Rinse and drain again. Combine the leeks, ¹/2 cup water, ¹/8 teaspoon salt and ¹/4 teaspoon pepper in a Dutch oven sprayed with butter-flavor nonstick cooking spray. Cook over medium-high heat for 10 minutes or until the leeks wilt, stirring occasionally. Spoon the leeks into a bowl.

Heat the olive oil in the Dutch oven over medium-high heat. Brown the pork on all sides in the hot oil for 5 minutes. Add the wine, ¹/8 teaspoon salt and ¹/4 teaspoon pepper to the Dutch oven. Cook for 15 seconds, scraping the bottom of the skillet constantly to release any browned bits. Return the leeks to the Dutch oven and mix well. Simmer, covered, for 2 hours or until the pork is cooked through, stirring occasionally. Remove the pork to a platter, reserving the leek mixture. Increase the heat and cook until the leek mixture is no longer watery if needed. Cut the pork into ¹/4-inch-thick slices. Serve the pork with the leek mixture. Garnish with parsley. **Yield:** 6 (3 ounces pork and 2¹/2 tablespoons leek mixture) servings.

Per Serving:
Calories: 242; Carbohydrate: 12.1 g; Protein: 24.8 g; Total Fat: 10.2 g;
Cholesterol: 67 mg; Sodium: 190 mg; Fiber: 1 g;
Calories from Fat: 37%

North African Lamb and Potato Kabobs

12 small red potatoes, cut into halves
4 garlic cloves, minced
1 tablespoon cumin
2 teaspoons olive oil
1 teaspoon oregano
1 teaspoon turmeric
1/2 teaspoon salt
1/2 teaspoon ginger
1/2 teaspoon cinnamon
1/8 teaspoon ground cloves
1 (2-pound) boneless leg of lamb, trimmed and cut into 48 cubes
2 large onions, each cut into 12 wedges

Combine the potatoes with enough water to cover in a saucepan. Bring to a boil; reduce the heat. Simmer for 12 minutes or until tender; drain. Combine the garlic, cumin, olive oil, oregano, turmeric, salt, ginger, cinnamon and cloves in a large bowl and mix well. Add the lamb to the garlic mixture and toss to coat. Marinate, covered, in the refrigerator for 20 minutes. Thread 4 lamb cubes, 2 potato halves and 2 onion wedges alternately on each of twelve 12-inch skewers. Arrange the skewers on a grill rack sprayed with nonstick cooking spray. Grill over hot coals for 4 minutes per side or until the lamb is the desired degree of doneness.
Yield: 8 (1 1/2-kabob) servings.

Per Serving:
Calories: 353; Carbohydrate: 31 g; Protein: 25.8 g; Total Fat: 13.7 g;
Cholesterol: 78 mg; Sodium: 216 mg; Fiber: 3.9 g;
Calories from Fat: 35%

Main Courses

Kofte or Kefta is a specialty of the Middle Eastern countries of the Mediterranean. By combining different spices, each country has their own version. Lean beef may be substituted for the lamb.

SPICY KOFTE

1 (1-pound) boneless leg of lamb, trimmed and cut into 1-inch cubes
3/4 cup chopped fresh parsley
3/4 cup chopped onion
1 (2-ounce) slice whole wheat nut bread, such as Arnold Health Nut
1/4 cup chopped fresh mint
5 garlic cloves
1 tablespoon red wine vinegar
1 teaspoon chili powder
1 teaspoon freshly ground pepper
1/4 teaspoon salt

Combine the lamb, parsley, onion, bread, mint, garlic, vinegar, chili powder, pepper and salt in a food processor. Process until smooth. Chill, covered, for 2 hours. Divide the lamb mixture into 6 equal portions. Shape each portion into a 6-inch log. Insert an 8-inch skewer through the center of each log. Arrange the skewers on a grill rack sprayed with nonstick cooking spray. Grill for 4 minutes per side or until cooked through. **Yield:** 6 servings.

PER SERVING:
CALORIES: 180; CARBOHYDRATE: 14.1 g; PROTEIN: 18.6 g; TOTAL FAT: 5.6 g;
CHOLESTEROL: 50 mg; SODIUM: 277 mg; FIBER: 2.6 g;
CALORIES FROM FAT: 28%

MARINATED SHISH KABOBS ✓

Marinade
3 large garlic cloves
2 tablespoons fresh lemon juice
2 tablespoons red wine vinegar or balsamic vinegar
2 tablespoons grated onion
1 tablespoon extra-virgin olive oil
1 bay leaf
1/4 teaspoon salt

Shish Kabobs
1 pound boneless lean sirloin steak or boneless leg of lamb,
trimmed and cut into 1¹/₂-inch cubes
2 large tomatoes, cut into quarters
2 green bell peppers, cut into 1-inch pieces
18 whole mushrooms
1 or 2 large onions, each cut into 8 wedges

For the marinade, combine the garlic, lemon juice, vinegar, onion, olive oil, bay leaf and salt in a bowl and mix well.

For the shish kabobs, mix the steak, tomatoes, bell peppers, mushrooms and onions in a shallow dish or sealable plastic bag. Pour the marinade over the steak mixture and toss to coat. Marinate, covered, in the refrigerator for 8 to 10 hours, stirring occasionally. Drain, reserving the marinade. Thread the steak alternately with the tomatoes, bell peppers, mushrooms and onions on six 12-inch skewers. Grill the skewers over medium-hot coals for 4 to 6 minutes per side or until the steak is the desired degree of doneness, basting frequently with the reserved marinade. **Yield:** 6 servings.

PER SERVING:
CALORIES: 230; CARBOHYDRATE: 10 g; PROTEIN: 24 g; TOTAL FAT: 8.6 g;
CHOLESTEROL: 58 mg; SODIUM: 154 mg; FIBER: 1.7 g;
CALORIES FROM FAT: 34%
Nutritional information includes the entire amount of the marinade.

MAIN COURSES

Accompaniments

If you look at the Mediterranean diet, you will see that the "side items" have a lot to do with the nutritional value of each meal.

The Mediterranean diet involves an abundance of food from plant sources—vegetables, fruits, breads, grains, beans, nuts, seeds, and herbs—with a low consumption of meat.

Vegetables are a great source of vitamins and minerals, along with the fiber we need to aid in digestion. A high content of vitamins can be found in many vegetables that are prevalent in the Mediterranean diet.

Unprocessed whole grains are a key ingredient, too. They are higher in fiber, especially water-soluble fiber, and are an important component of a heart healthy diet.

So you know mom was right: Vegetables are good for you and don't forget the whole grains and legumes. Let us show you just how good they can taste.

Italian Asparagus

1 pound fresh asparagus spears
3/4 cup chopped tomato
2 tablespoons chopped green onions
1/8 teaspoon whole oregano
1/8 teaspoon basil
1/8 teaspoon pepper
2 teaspoons freshly grated Parmesan cheese

Snap off the woody ends of the asparagus spears and discard. Remove the scales from the spears with a knife or vegetable peeler if desired. Place the asparagus in a vegetable steamer over boiling water. Steam, covered, for 4 to 5 minutes or until tender-crisp. Arrange the asparagus on a serving platter and cover to keep warm. Combine the tomato, green onions, oregano, basil and pepper in a bowl and mix well. Spoon the tomato mixture over the asparagus and sprinkle with the cheese.
Yield: 4 servings.

Per Serving:
Calories: 28; Carbohydrate: 4.6 g; Protein: 2.8 g; Total Fat: 0.6 g;
Cholesterol: 1 mg; Sodium: 24 mg; Fiber: 2 g;
Calories from Fat: 19%

ACCOMPANIMENTS

Broccoli with Feta Sauce

2 tablespoons minced onion
1¹/2 cups evaporated skim milk or fat-free half-and-half
2 tablespoons water
1¹/2 tablespoons cornstarch
2 ounces feta cheese, crumbled
¹/8 teaspoon salt
2 tablespoons lemon juice
¹/2 teaspoon whole dill weed
4 cups broccoli florets
Lemon zest (optional)

Spray a saucepan with nonstick cooking spray and heat over medium-high heat. Sauté the onion in the hot saucepan for 4 minutes or until tender. Add the evaporated skim milk to the saucepan gradually, stirring constantly. Cook for 5 minutes, stirring frequently; do not allow the mixture to boil. Mix the water and cornstarch in a small bowl until blended. Add the cornstarch mixture to the milk mixture and mix well. Cook until slightly thickened, stirring constantly. Stir in the cheese and salt. Cook until heated through, stirring constantly. Remove from the heat. Stir in the lemon juice and dill weed. Cover to keep warm. Place the broccoli in a vegetable steamer over boiling water. Steam, covered, for 5 minutes or until tender-crisp. Remove the broccoli to a serving bowl. Spoon the cheese sauce over the broccoli and garnish with lemon zest. Serve immediately. **Yield:** 4 (1-cup) servings.

Per Serving:
Calories: 147; Carbohydrate: 18.7 g; Protein: 11.3 g; Total Fat: 3.6 g;
Cholesterol: 16 mg; Sodium: 360 mg; Fiber: 2.7 g;
Calories from Fat: 22%

Try using frozen chopped onions in recipes for soups, stews, and other sauces. There is no need to thaw first.

Accompaniments

125

To use fresh herbs in a recipe that calls for dried herbs, triple the amount specified.

GRILLED SQUASH FANS WITH ROMA TOMATOES

6 yellow squash
3 Roma tomatoes
1/2 cup fat-free Italian dressing
3 garlic cloves, crushed
2 tablespoons chopped fresh basil
1 teaspoon pepper

Cut each squash lengthwise to within 1 inch of the stem into 1/4-inch slices to form a fan. Cut the tomatoes into 1/4-inch slices. Mix the dressing and garlic in a large shallow dish. Add the squash and tomatoes to the dressing mixture and toss gently. Marinate at room temperature for 1 hour, turning occasionally. Remove the squash and tomatoes from the marinade, reserving the marinade. Sprinkle the basil and pepper over the squash and tomatoes. Insert the tomato slices between the squash slices and secure with wooden skewers. Arrange on a grill rack sprayed with nonstick cooking spray. Grill with the lid down over medium-high heat for 8 minutes per side or until tender-crisp, basting with the reserved marinade as desired. **Yield:** 6 servings.

PER SERVING:
CALORIES: 34; CARBOHYDRATE: 7.3 g; PROTEIN: 1.2 g; TOTAL FAT: 0.4 g;
CHOLESTEROL: 0 mg; SODIUM: 194 mg; FIBER: 1.5 g;
CALORIES FROM FAT: 2%
Nutritional information includes the entire amount of the marinade.

ACCOMPANIMENTS

Hortarika Piata

1 pound summer squash ♦ 1 pound fresh green beans, trimmed
1 large onion, finely chopped ♦ 1 tablespoon olive oil
2 garlic cloves, finely chopped ♦ 2 cups water
1 (8-ounce) can tomato sauce ♦ ¼ teaspoon salt ♦ ¼ teaspoon pepper

Cut each squash lengthwise into 3 slices. Leave the green beans long, or no shorter than 3 inches. Spray a large skillet with nonstick cooking spray. Sauté the onion, olive oil and garlic in the prepared skillet until the onion is tender. Stir in the water and tomato sauce. Stir the squash, beans, salt and pepper into the tomato sauce mixture. Simmer, covered, until the vegetables are tender, stirring occasionally. **Yield:** 6 servings.

Per Serving:
Calories: 103; Carbohydrate: 13 g; Protein: 2.7 g; Total Fat: 2.3 g;
Cholesterol: 0 mg; Sodium: 106 mg; Fiber: 2.6 g;
Calories from Fat: 20%

Oven-Dried Tomatoes

12 Roma tomatoes ♦ 1 tablespoon balsamic vinegar
2 teaspoons finely chopped fresh thyme
½ teaspoon freshly ground pepper ♦ ¼ teaspoon kosher salt

Cut the tomatoes lengthwise into halves. Combine the vinegar, thyme, pepper and kosher salt in a bowl and mix well. Add the tomatoes to the vinegar mixture and toss gently until coated. Arrange the tomatoes cut side up on a baking sheet sprayed with olive oil-flavor nonstick cooking spray. Spray the tomatoes with olive oil-flavor nonstick cooking spray. Bake at 200 degrees for 6 to 8 hours. The tomatoes will be slightly shriveled and golden red in color at the end of the baking process. **Yield:** 12 (2-tomato half) servings.

Per Serving:
Calories: 13; Carbohydrate: 2.8 g; Protein: 0.5 g; Total Fat: 0 g;
Cholesterol: 0 mg; Sodium: 46 mg; Fiber: 0.7 g;
Calories from Fat: 0%

Accompaniments

Roasted Tomatoes with Shallots and Herbs

4 medium tomatoes, cut horizontally into halves, cored and seeded
1/2 teaspoon salt ◆ 1/4 cup minced shallots or red onion
1 tablespoon chopped fresh flat-leaf parsley
1 teaspoon chopped fresh oregano ◆ 1 teaspoon chopped fresh thyme
1/2 teaspoon chopped fresh rosemary
1/4 teaspoon freshly ground pepper ◆ 2 teaspoons olive oil

Sprinkle the cut sides of the tomato halves with 1/4 teaspoon of the salt; drain for 20 minutes. Arrange the tomato halves cut sides up in a 9×13-inch baking dish sprayed with nonstick cooking spray. Sprinkle with the remaining 1/4 teaspoon salt, shallots, parsley, oregano, thyme, rosemary and pepper. Drizzle with the olive oil. Bake at 350 degrees for 15 to 20 minutes or until tender. **Yield:** 8 (1-tomato half) servings.

Per Serving:
Calories: 38; Carbohydrate: 6.2 g; Protein: 1.1 g; Total Fat: 1.5 g;
Cholesterol: 0 mg; Sodium: 121 mg; Fiber: 1.3 g;
Calories from Fat: 36%

Rapid Ratatouille

5 cups sliced zucchini
1 (28-ounce) can whole tomatoes, drained and coarsely chopped
1 1/2 cups vertically sliced onions ◆ 1 cup green bell pepper strips
1 teaspoon Italian seasoning ◆ Grated Parmesan cheese (optional)

Mix the vegetables and Italian seasoning in a microwave-safe dish. Microwave, covered, on High for 7 minutes; stir. Microwave for 7 minutes; stir. Serve with Parmesan cheese. **Yield:** 6 (1-cup) servings.

Per Serving:
Calories: 48; Carbohydrate: 10.7 g; Protein: 2.5 g; Total Fat: 0.3 g;
Cholesterol: 0 mg; Sodium: 329 mg; Fiber: 3.5 g;
Calories from Fat: 6%

ACCOMPANIMENTS

Polenta with Fontina Cheese and Spinach

2 garlic cloves, minced
3 cups chopped trimmed fresh spinach
2 cups water
1 (14-ounce) can fat-free less-sodium chicken broth
1 cup polenta
1/8 teaspoon salt
1/4 teaspoon pepper
1/2 cup (2 ounces) shredded fontina cheese or Parmesan cheese

Heat a medium nonstick skillet sprayed with olive oil-flavor nonstick cooking spray over medium-high heat. Sauté the garlic in the hot skillet for 1 minute. Add the spinach. Sauté for 1 minute or until the spinach wilts. Remove from the heat. Combine the water and broth in a large saucepan over medium-high heat. Bring to a boil. Add the polenta to the broth mixture gradually, whisking constantly. Reduce the heat to medium. Cook for 20 minutes, stirring frequently. Remove from the heat. Stir in the spinach mixture, salt and pepper.

Spoon the polenta into a 9-inch springform pan sprayed with olive oil-flavor nonstick cooking spray. Press plastic wrap over the surface of the polenta. Chill for 2 hours or until firm. Remove the polenta from the pan and place on a baking sheet coated with olive oil-flavor nonstick cooking spray. Sprinkle the cheese over the top. Bake at 400 degrees for 15 minutes or until the cheese melts and begins to brown. Remove from the oven. Let stand for 5 minutes and cut into wedges with a sharp knife. Serve immediately. **Yield:** 8 (1-wedge) servings.

Per Serving:
Calories: 126; Carbohydrate: 16.9 g; Protein: 5.7 g; Total Fat: 4.2 g;
Cholesterol: 9 mg; Sodium: 311 mg; Fiber: 1.9 g;
Calories from Fat: 30%

Add salt substitute after the food is cooked because cooking with a salt substitute will make the food taste bitter.

Accompaniments

Baked Risotto with Asparagus, Spinach and Parmesan Cheese

1 tablespoon olive oil
1 cup finely chopped onion
1 cup arborio rice
8 cups trimmed fresh spinach leaves (about 4 ounces)
2 cups fat-free less-sodium chicken broth
1/4 teaspoon nutmeg (optional)
1/2 cup (2 ounces) freshly grated Parmesan cheese
1 1/2 cups (1-inch) diagonal slices fresh asparagus

Heat the olive oil in a Dutch oven over medium heat. Cook the onion in the hot oil for 4 minutes or until tender, stirring frequently. Stir in the rice. Add the spinach, broth and nutmeg and mix well. Bring to a simmer. Simmer for 7 minutes, stirring occasionally. Stir in 1/4 cup of the cheese. Bake, covered, at 400 degrees for 15 minutes. Stir in the asparagus and sprinkle with the remaining 1/4 cup cheese. Bake, covered, for 15 minutes longer or until the liquid is almost absorbed.
Yield: 4 (1-cup) servings.

Per Serving:
Calories: 309; Carbohydrate: 47.6 g; Protein: 12.3 g; Total Fat: 7.6 g;
Cholesterol: 10 mg; Sodium: 411 mg; Fiber: 3.7 g;
Calories from Fat: 22%

ACCOMPANIMENTS

CREAMY RISOTTO

2³/4 cups fat-free less-sodium chicken broth
1¹/2 teaspoons olive oil
3 tablespoons finely chopped onion
³/4 cup arborio rice or other short grain rice
3 tablespoons dry white wine
2 tablespoons freshly grated Parmesan cheese
1 tablespoon minced fresh parsley

Bring the broth to a simmer in a medium saucepan; do not boil. Keep warm over low heat. Heat the olive oil in a large Dutch oven over medium-high heat. Sauté the onion in the hot oil for 3 minutes. Stir in the rice. Sauté for 1 minute. Stir in the wine. Cook for 1 minute or until the liquid is nearly absorbed, stirring constantly. Add ¹/2 cup of the warm broth and mix well. Cook until the liquid is absorbed, stirring constantly. Add the remaining warm broth ¹/2 cup at a time, cooking until the liquid has been absorbed after each addition and stirring constantly. This process should take approximately 20 minutes. Remove from the heat. Stir in the cheese and parsley. **Yield:** 2 (1-cup) servings.

PER SERVING:
CALORIES: 345; CARBOHYDRATE: 56.5 g; PROTEIN: 7.5 g; TOTAL FAT: 5.1 g;
CHOLESTEROL: 3 mg; SODIUM: 109 mg; FIBER: 1.3 g;
CALORIES FROM FAT: 13%

ACCOMPANIMENTS

Risotto is traditionally made with arborio rice or short grain rice because of its high starch content and firm texture. Constant stirring helps release the starch from the rice, creating a creamy texture yet leaving each grain of rice separate.

LEMON RISOTTO WITH ASPARAGUS

3 (14-ounce) cans fat-free less-sodium chicken broth
1 tablespoon olive oil
1/2 cup finely chopped onion
1 1/2 cups arborio rice
2 teaspoons grated lemon zest
1/2 cup dry white wine
3 cups (1-inch) diagonal slices fresh asparagus (about 1 pound)
1/2 cup (2 ounces) grated Parmigiano-Reggiano cheese
2 tablespoons fresh lemon juice
2 teaspoons fresh thyme leaves

Bring the broth to a simmer in a large saucepan; do not boil. Keep warm over low heat. Heat the olive oil in a large nonstick skillet over medium heat. Cook the onion in the hot oil for 5 minutes or until tender, stirring frequently. Add the rice and lemon zest and mix well. Cook for 2 minutes, stirring constantly. Stir in the wine. Cook for 3 minutes or until the liquid is almost absorbed, stirring constantly. Add 3 1/2 cups of the broth 1/2 cup at a time, stirring constantly until each addition is absorbed before adding the next portion. This process will take approximately 20 minutes. Stir in the asparagus. Add the remaining broth 1/2 cup at a time, stirring constantly until each addition of the broth is absorbed before adding the next addition. This process will take approximately 10 minutes. Remove from the heat. Stir in the cheese and lemon juice and sprinkle with the thyme. Serve immediately. **Yield:** 8 (1-cup) servings.

PER SERVING:
CALORIES: 230; CARBOHYDRATE: 38.4 g; PROTEIN: 8.7 g; TOTAL FAT: 3.7 g;
CHOLESTEROL: 4.5 mg; SODIUM: 399 mg; FIBER: 2 g;
CALORIES FROM FAT: 14%

ACCOMPANIMENTS

Wild Mushroom and Barley Risotto

1/4 cup dried porcini mushrooms
1 1/2 cups boiling water
2 cups fat-free less-sodium chicken broth
2 tablespoons olive oil
1/4 cup minced shallots or red onion
1 cup pearl barley
1 1/2 teaspoons chopped fresh thyme or rosemary, or
1/2 teaspoon dried thyme or rosemary
Freshly ground pepper to taste

Combine the mushrooms and boiling water in a heatproof bowl. Let stand for 30 minutes or until the mushrooms are soft. Cool slightly and remove the mushrooms to a bowl using a slotted spoon and reserving the liquid. Chop the mushrooms. Strain the reserved liquid through cheesecloth into a small saucepan. Add the mushrooms and broth to the reserved liquid. Bring to a boil over high heat; reduce the heat. Keep the broth mixture warm over low heat. Heat the olive oil in a large saucepan over medium heat. Sauté the shallots in the hot oil for 3 to 4 minutes or until the shallots are tender. Stir in the barley. Sauté for 1 minute. Stir in 1/2 cup of the broth mixture. Cook over low heat until the liquid is absorbed, stirring constantly. Add the remaining broth mixture 1/2 cup at a time, stirring constantly until each addition of the liquid is absorbed before adding the next addition. This process will take approximately 30 to 35 minutes. Stir in the thyme and pepper.
Yield: 6 (1/2-cup) servings.

Per Serving:
Calories: 188; Carbohydrate: 30 g; Protein: 6.3 g; Total Fat: 5.1 g;
Cholesterol: 0 mg; Sodium: 213 mg; Fiber: 6.2 g;
Calories from Fat: 16%

Accompaniments

WILD RICE AND QUINOA PILAF

1 tablespoon olive oil
1/3 cup finely chopped onion
1/3 cup finely chopped celery
1/3 cup finely chopped carrots
1/4 cup chopped red bell pepper
2 garlic cloves, minced
1 cup quinoa, rinsed and drained
1/4 cup pistachio nuts or almonds, chopped
3 cups fat-free less-sodium chicken broth or vegetable broth
1 cup cooked wild rice
Freshly ground pepper to taste

Heat the olive oil in a saucepan over medium heat. Sauté the onion, celery, carrots, bell pepper and garlic in the hot oil until the vegetables begin to soften. Stir in the quinoa and pistachio nuts. Cook for 1 to 2 minutes, stirring frequently. Add the broth and mix well. Bring to a boil; reduce the heat. Simmer, covered, for 18 to 20 minutes, stirring occasionally. Stir in the wild rice. Simmer, covered, for 2 to 3 minutes or until heated through, stirring occasionally. Taste and adjust seasonings. Stir in the pepper. If time is of the essence, cook the wild rice using package directions the night before and store, covered, in the refrigerator. **Yield:** 10 (1/2-cup) servings.

PER SERVING:
CALORIES: 165; CARBOHYDRATE: 26 g; PROTEIN: 6.2 g; TOTAL FAT: 4.8 g;
CHOLESTEROL: 0 mg; SODIUM: 228 mg; FIBER: 2.6 g;
CALORIES FROM FAT: 26%

ACCOMPANIMENTS

Mediterranean Lemon Couscous

1¹/4 cups water
³/4 cup couscous
¹/4 cup sliced green onions
2 tablespoons finely chopped fresh parsley
2 tablespoons orange juice
1 tablespoon fresh lemon juice
1 teaspoon grated lemon zest
¹/8 teaspoon salt
¹/8 teaspoon pepper

Bring the water to a boil in a medium saucepan. Add the couscous gradually, stirring constantly. Remove from the heat. Let stand, covered, for 5 minutes; fluff with a fork. Add the green onions, parsley, orange juice, lemon juice, lemon zest, salt and pepper to the couscous and mix well. **Yield:** 4 (¹/2-cup) servings.

Per Serving:
Calories: 102; Carbohydrate: 21.8 g; Protein: 3.7 g; Total Fat: 0.3 g;
Cholesterol: 0 mg; Sodium: 79 mg; Fiber: 1.3 g;
Calories from Fat: 3%

Accompaniments

ACCOMPANIMENTS

PASTA WITH BASIL, ARUGULA AND WALNUT PESTO

2 cups fresh basil leaves
2 cups arugula leaves
1/4 cup fresh flat-leaf parsley leaves
3 tablespoons walnuts
2 tablespoons olive oil
4 garlic cloves
1/2 cup (2 ounces) grated Parmigiano-Reggiano cheese
1/3 cup fat-free less-sodium chicken broth
1/2 teaspoon freshly ground pepper
1/4 teaspoon salt
8 cups hot cooked linguini (about 16 ounces)

Combine the basil, arugula, parsley, walnuts, olive oil and garlic in a food processor. Pulse 7 or 8 times or until the mixture is of a paste consistency. Add the cheese, broth, pepper and salt. Pulse until combined. Combine the pesto and hot pasta in a large bowl and toss to coat. **Yield:** 6 (1 1/3-cup) servings.

PER SERVING:
CALORIES: 320; CARBOHYDRATE: 44 g; PROTEIN: 12.7 g; TOTAL FAT: 11.3 g;
CHOLESTEROL: 7.3 mg; SODIUM: 431 mg; FIBER: 3.2 g;
CALORIES FROM FAT: 32%

Mediterranean Pasta

16 ounces pasta of choice
2 (14-ounce) cans no-salt-added Italian tomatoes
1 onion, finely chopped
1½ teaspoons olive oil
3 garlic cloves, minced
2 tablespoons finely chopped fresh basil, or 1 tablespoon dried basil
¼ cup pitted black olives, sliced
¼ teaspoon pepper
⅛ teaspoon salt
¼ cup (1 ounce) freshly grated Parmesan cheese

Cook the pasta using package directions without added fat or salt; drain. Cover to keep warm. Process the tomatoes in a blender for 2 to 3 seconds or until coarsely chopped. Sauté the onion in the olive oil in a saucepan for 2 to 3 minutes; do not brown. Stir in the garlic. Sauté for 5 minutes or until the onion is tender. Add the tomatoes and basil to the onion mixture and mix well. Simmer for 30 to 40 minutes, stirring occasionally. Stir in the olives, pepper and salt. Cook until heated through, stirring frequently. Divide the pasta evenly among 4 serving plates. Spoon ¼ of the sauce over each serving and top each with 1 tablespoon of the cheese. Serve immediately. **Yield:** 4 servings.

Per Serving:
Calories: 289; Carbohydrate: 48 g; Protein: 11 g; Total Fat: 7.8 g;
Cholesterol: 5 mg; Sodium: 322 mg; Fiber: 1.8 g;
Calories from Fat: 24%

Accompaniments

Breads and Spreads

Bread is the universal food, the primary food source for all cultures since time began. In the Mediterranean, no meal is complete without it. Mediterranean breads come in all shapes and sizes, and can be baked with many types of herbs and olive oil.

From pita bread, often stuffed to make a filling lunch, to Tuscany bread, which contains tomatoes, sweet peppers, herbs, and olives, there are breads here for every taste. Combined with traditional Mediterranean spreads, such as hummus, olive oil, baba ghanouj, or an olive tapanade, they are almost a meal in themselves.

We hope you enjoy the following variations on the universal food and the spreads that go with them.

*The cultivation of olives
dates back more than five
thousand years. The color
of an olive depends on the
stage at which it was
harvested. Green olives have
the firmest flesh, as they are
first to be picked. As green
olives mature, they turn
purple, then black.*

OLIVE BREAD

1 (1-pound) loaf frozen whole wheat bread dough
1/2 cup chopped pitted kalamata olives
1 1/2 teaspoons dried rosemary, or
1 tablespoon chopped fresh rosemary
1 egg white, lightly beaten

Thaw the bread dough in the refrigerator for 12 hours. Sprinkle the olives and rosemary over the dough. Knead gently 4 or 5 times on a lightly floured surface or just until the olives are incorporated into the dough. Let rest, covered, for 10 minutes. Roll the dough into an 8×10-inch rectangle. Roll as for a jelly roll beginning with the long side; pinch the seam to seal. Arrange the loaf seam side down on a baking sheet sprayed with nonstick cooking spray. Let rise, covered, in a warm place (85 degrees) free from drafts for 1 hour or until doubled in bulk. Make several 2-inch diagonal slits in the top of the dough with a sharp knife and brush with the egg white. Bake at 375 degrees for 40 minutes or until the loaf sounds hollow when lightly tapped. Remove the loaf to a wire rack to cool. **Yield:** 12 (1-slice) servings.

PER SERVING:
CALORIES: 96; CARBOHYDRATE: 16.4 g; PROTEIN: 3.3 g; TOTAL FAT: 1.9 g;
CHOLESTEROL: 0 mg; SODIUM: 226 mg; FIBER: 1.2 g;
CALORIES FROM FAT: 18%

BREADS AND
SPREADS

SPINACH AND FETA BREAD

1 (1-pound) loaf frozen whole wheat bread dough
1 (10-ounce) package frozen chopped spinach, thawed and drained
1 (14-ounce) can artichoke hearts, drained and chopped
1/2 cup (2 ounces) crumbled feta cheese
1/3 cup 1/3-less-fat cream cheese, softened
3 garlic cloves, minced
1 egg white, lightly beaten
1/2 teaspoon basil
1/2 teaspoon oregano
1/4 teaspoon pepper
2 tablespoons (1/2 ounce) freshly grated Parmesan cheese

Thaw the bread dough in the refrigerator for 12 hours. Press the excess moisture from the spinach. Combine the spinach, artichokes, feta cheese, cream cheese, garlic, egg white, basil, oregano and pepper in a bowl and mix well. Roll the dough into a 10×16-inch rectangle on a lightly floured surface. Spread the spinach mixture over the rectangle to within 1/2 inch of the sides. Roll as for a jelly roll beginning with the long side and pinch the seam and ends to seal. Arrange the loaf seam side down on a baking sheet sprayed with nonstick cooking spray. Make diagonal slits in the top of the loaf using a sharp knife. Let rise, covered, in a warm place (85 degrees) free from drafts for 1 hour or until doubled in bulk. Sprinkle the Parmesan cheese over the top of the loaf. Bake at 350 degrees for 45 minutes or until the loaf is golden brown. Remove the loaf to a wire rack to cool. **Yield:** 16 (1-slice) servings.

PER SERVING:
CALORIES: 137; CARBOHYDRATE: 21.5 g; PROTEIN: 5.9 g; TOTAL FAT: 2.9 g;
CHOLESTEROL: 11 mg; SODIUM: 385 mg; FIBER: 2.2 g;
CALORIES FROM FAT: 19%

BREADS AND
SPREADS

Avoid rinsing mushrooms, if at all possible, as they soak up water. To clean, wipe the mushrooms with a damp cloth or paper towels, scratching off any particles of dirt left with a small knife and cutting away any unwanted parts.

ROSEMARY ROLLS

1 (1-pound) loaf frozen whole wheat bread dough
1 cup finely chopped fresh mushrooms
1/4 cup chopped shallots or red onion
2 teaspoons olive oil
1 1/2 tablespoons chopped fresh basil, or 1 1/2 teaspoons dried basil
1 teaspoon rosemary
3/4 cup roasted red and yellow bell peppers, coarsely chopped
2 teaspoons red wine vinegar
1/4 to 1/2 teaspoon crushed red pepper flakes
1/8 teaspoon salt
1/4 cup (1 ounce) freshly grated Parmesan cheese
1 teaspoon olive oil

Thaw the bread dough in the refrigerator for 12 hours. Combine the mushrooms, shallots and 2 teaspoons olive oil in a nonstick skillet. Cook over medium heat for 2 to 3 minutes or until the shallots begin to soften, stirring constantly. Stir in the basil and rosemary. Cook for 1 minute, stirring constantly. Remove from the heat. Stir in the roasted peppers, vinegar and red pepper flakes. Mix in the salt. Taste and adjust the seasonings.

Roll the dough into a 9×12-inch rectangle on a lightly floured surface. Spread the mushroom mixture over the rectangle to within 1/2 inch of the edges. Sprinkle with 2 tablespoons of the cheese. Roll the dough lengthwise and pinch the ends to seal. Cut the roll into twelve 1-inch slices with a serrated knife. Arrange the slices cut side up on a baking sheet sprayed lightly with nonstick cooking spray. Brush the tops of the slices with 1 teaspoon olive oil. Let rise, covered with plastic wrap, in a warm place (85 degrees) free from drafts for 30 minutes or until doubled in bulk. Sprinkle with the remaining 2 tablespoons cheese. Bake at 325 degrees for 20 to 25 minutes or until golden brown. Serve warm or at room temperature. **Yield:** 12 (1-roll) servings.

PER SERVING:
CALORIES: 144; CARBOHYDRATE: 20.6 g; PROTEIN: 5.7 g; TOTAL FAT: 3.4 g;
CHOLESTEROL: 1.6 mg; SODIUM: 177 mg; FIBER: 1.8 g;
CALORIES FROM FAT: 21%

BREADS AND
SPREADS

Flatbread with Oven-Dried Tomatoes and Fontina Cheese

4 sprigs of rosemary ♦ 2 tablespoons olive oil
2³/4 cups flour ♦ 1 envelope dry yeast
1 cup plus 2 tablespoons very warm (120 to 130 degrees) water
2 teaspoons chopped fresh rosemary, or ¹/2 teaspoon dried rosemary
¹/4 teaspoon salt
³/4 cup Oven-Dried Tomatoes, cut lengthwise into halves (page 127)
1 cup (4 ounces) cubed fontina cheese

Combine the rosemary sprigs and olive oil in a small microwave-safe bowl. Microwave on High for 30 seconds. Let stand for 15 minutes. Gently squeeze the oil from the rosemary and discard the sprigs. Lightly spoon the flour into dry measuring cups and level with a knife. Combine ¹/2 cup of the flour and yeast in a large bowl and stir with a whisk. Stir in ¹/2 cup of the warm water. Let stand for 20 minutes. Add the rosemary oil, 2 cups of the flour, the remaining ¹/2 cup plus 2 tablespoons warm water, chopped fresh rosemary and salt to the yeast mixture and stir until a soft dough forms.

Knead the dough on a lightly floured surface for 8 minutes or until smooth and elastic, adding enough of the remaining ¹/4 cup flour 1 teaspoon at a time to prevent the dough from sticking to hands; the dough will feel tacky. Place the dough in a large bowl sprayed with nonstick cooking spray and turn to coat. Let rise, covered, in a warm place (85 degrees) free from drafts for 1 hour or until doubled in bulk. Press 2 fingers into the dough. If the indentation remains, the dough has risen enough. Punch the dough down and shape into a ball. Place the ball on a baking sheet. Let rest for 5 minutes. Roll the ball into a 12-inch round. Arrange the tomatoes over the surface of the round to within ¹/2 inch of the edge and sprinkle with the cheese; gently press the toppings into the dough. Bake at 500 degrees for 10 minutes or until golden brown. **Yield:** 12 (1-wedge) servings.

Per Serving:
Calories: 162; Carbohydrate: 24.2 g; Protein: 6 g; Total Fat: 4.5 g;
Cholesterol: 11 mg; Sodium: 191 mg; Fiber: 1.4 g;
Calories from Fat: 25%

Breads and
Spreads

ROSEMARY FLATBREAD WITH GRAPES

3¹/₄ cups bread flour ◆ 1 envelope dry yeast
1 teaspoon sugar ◆ 1¹/₄ cups warm (100 to 110 degrees) water
¹/₂ cup white cornmeal
1¹/₂ teaspoons chopped fresh rosemary
2¹/₂ teaspoons olive oil ◆ ¹/₂ teaspoon salt
1 cup seedless black grapes, cut into quarters
Sprigs of fresh rosemary (optional)

Lightly spoon the bread flour into dry measuring cups and level with a knife. Dissolve the yeast and sugar in the warm water in a large bowl and mix well. Stir in 1 cup of the bread flour. Let stand, loosely covered with plastic wrap, for 30 minutes. Add 2 cups of the bread flour, cornmeal, chopped rosemary, 1¹/₂ teaspoons of the olive oil and salt to the yeast mixture and stir until a soft dough forms. Knead the dough on a lightly floured surface for 8 minutes or until smooth and elastic, adding enough of the remaining ¹/₄ cup bread flour 1 teaspoon at a time to prevent the dough from sticking to hands; the dough will feel tacky. Place the dough in a large bowl sprayed with nonstick cooking spray and turn to coat. Let rise, covered, in a warm place (85 degrees) free from drafts for 1 hour or until doubled in bulk. Press 2 fingers into the dough. If the indentation remains, the dough has risen enough.

Punch the dough down and place on a lightly floured surface. Arrange ²/₃ cup of the grapes over the dough and knead gently 4 or 5 times or just until the grapes are incorporated into the dough. Let rest for 5 minutes. Pat the dough into a 10×15-inch rectangle on a baking sheet sprayed with nonstick cooking spray. Brush the surface with the remaining 1 teaspoon olive oil. Let rise, covered, for 30 minutes or until doubled in bulk. Make indentations in the top of the rectangle using the handle of a wooden spoon or fingertips. Sprinkle with the remaining ¹/₃ cup grapes and press gently. Bake at 475 degrees for 20 minutes or until golden brown. Garnish with sprigs of rosemary. **Yield:** 12 servings.

PER SERVING:
CALORIES: 164; CARBOHYDRATE: 33 g; PROTEIN: 4.4 g; TOTAL FAT: 1.4 g;
CHOLESTEROL: 0 mg; SODIUM: 102 mg; FIBER: 1.6 g;
CALORIES FROM FAT: 8%

Red Onion Focaccia

Sponge
1 envelope dry yeast ♦ 1 teaspoon honey
2 cups warm (100 to 110 degrees) water
2 cups all-purpose flour

Focaccia and Toppings
1 cup bread flour ♦ 1 cup whole wheat flour
5 teaspoons olive oil
3/4 teaspoon salt ♦ 5 cups thinly sliced red onions
1 tablespoon chopped fresh rosemary
1/8 teaspoon salt
1/4 teaspoon crushed red pepper

For the sponge, dissolve the yeast and honey in the warm water in a large bowl and mix well. Let stand for 5 minutes. Lightly spoon the all-purpose flour into dry measuring cups and level with a knife. Stir the all-purpose flour into the yeast mixture. Chill, covered, for 8 to 10 hours.

For the focaccia, lightly spoon the flours into dry measuring cups and level with a knife. Combine the yeast mixture, bread flour, whole wheat flour, 3 teaspoons of the olive oil and 3/4 teaspoon salt in a mixing bowl. Beat at medium speed for 15 minutes or until the dough pulls from the side of the bowl. Let rise, covered, in a warm place (85 degrees) free from drafts for 1 hour or until doubled in bulk; the dough will be wet. Brush 1 teaspoon of the olive oil over the bottom of a 10×15-inch baking pan. Pour the dough into the prepared pan. Let stand for 5 minutes. Press the dough gently to cover the pan. Let stand for 30 minutes. Heat the remaining 1 teaspoon olive oil in a large nonstick skillet over medium heat. Cook the onions and rosemary in the hot oil for 15 minutes or until the onions are brown, stirring frequently. Spoon the onion mixture over the dough. Sprinkle with 1/8 teaspoon salt and red pepper. Bake at 425 degrees for 25 minutes or until golden brown. Let stand for 5 minutes before slicing. **Yield:** 12 servings.

PER SERVING:
CALORIES: 197; CARBOHYDRATE: 38 g; PROTEIN: 5.9 g; TOTAL FAT: 2.6 g;
CHOLESTEROL: 0 mg; SODIUM: 162 mg; FIBER: 3.4 g;
CALORIES FROM FAT: 12%

BREADS AND
SPREADS

Rosemary Focaccia

Sponge
1 teaspoon honey ◆ 1 envelope dry yeast
1¼ cups warm (100 to 110 degrees) water
1½ cups all-purpose flour
2 tablespoons extra-virgin olive oil

Focaccia and Toppings
1 cup all-purpose flour ◆ ½ cup whole wheat flour
½ teaspoon salt
1 teaspoon chopped fresh rosemary
1 tablespoon olive oil
1 tablespoon fresh rosemary leaves
¼ teaspoon kosher salt

For the sponge, dissolve the honey and yeast in the warm water in a large mixing bowl and mix well. Let stand for 5 minutes. Lightly spoon the all-purpose flour into dry measuring cups and level with a knife. Stir the all-purpose flour and olive oil into the yeast mixture. Let rise, covered, in a warm place (85 degrees) free from drafts for 1 hour.

For the focaccia, lightly spoon the flours into dry measuring cups and level with a knife. Stir the all-purpose flour, whole wheat flour, ½ teaspoon salt and chopped rosemary into the yeast mixture. Beat at medium speed for 6 minutes or until the dough is smooth and elastic; the dough will be sticky. Let rise, covered, in a warm place (85 degrees) free from drafts for 1½ hours or until doubled in bulk; the dough will be wet. Pat the dough into an 8×12-inch rectangle on a 10×15-inch baking pan sprayed with nonstick cooking spray. Brush the surface with the olive oil and sprinkle with fresh rosemary leaves and ¼ teaspoon kosher salt. Let rise, covered, for 30 minutes. Bake at 400 degrees for 25 minutes or until golden brown. Let stand for 5 minutes before slicing. **Yield:** 10 servings.

Per Serving:
Calories: 175; Carbohydrate: 29.2 g; Protein: 4.4 g; Total Fat: 4.5 g;
Cholesterol: 0 mg; Sodium: 157 mg; Fiber: 1.9 g;
Calories from Fat: 23%

Breads and
Spreads

Quick and Easy Pizza Crust

2 cups bread flour
1 envelope fast-rising yeast
1/2 teaspoon sugar ♦ 1/4 teaspoon salt
3/4 cup warm (120 to 130 degrees) water
1 tablespoon olive oil ♦ 2 tablespoons cornmeal

Lightly spoon the bread flour into dry measuring cups and level with a knife. Combine the bread flour, yeast, sugar and salt in a large bowl and mix well. Make a well in the center of the flour mixture. Mix the warm water and olive oil in a small bowl. Add the water mixture to the well and mix until the mixture forms a ball. Knead the dough on a lightly floured surface for 10 minutes or until smooth and elastic. Place the dough in a large bowl sprayed with nonstick cooking spray and turn to coat. Let rise in a warm place (85 degrees) free from drafts for 45 minutes or until doubled in bulk. Punch the dough down. Divide the dough into 2 equal portions. Let rest, covered, for 10 minutes. Working with 1 portion at a time and keeping the remaining portion covered to prevent drying out, roll each into a 10-inch round on a lightly floured surface. Arrange the round on a baking sheet sprinkled with 1 tablespoon of the cornmeal. Repeat the process with the remaining dough and remaining cornmeal. **Yield:** 8 servings.

Food Processor Variation: Combine the flour, yeast, sugar and salt in a food processor. Pulse 2 times or until blended. Add the water and oil gradually, processing constantly until the mixture forms a ball. Process for 1 minute longer. Knead the dough 9 or 10 times on a lightly floured surface. Place the dough in a bowl sprayed with nonstick cooking spray. Proceed as directed above. *Bread Machine Variation:* Follow the manufacturer's instructions for placing all ingredients except the cornmeal in the bread pan. Set the bread machine on the dough cycle. Remove the dough from the machine and place in a bowl sprayed with nonstick cooking spray. Proceed as directed above.

PER SERVING:
CALORIES: 151; CARBOHYDRATE: 27 g; PROTEIN: 4.6 g; TOTAL FAT: 2.4 g;
CHOLESTEROL: 0 mg; SODIUM: 72 mg; FIBER: .04 g;
CALORIES FROM FAT: 14%

BREADS AND
SPREADS

A fougasse (FOO-gahss) is a French bread shaped by slashing the dough and stretching it to resemble a ladder or tree-of-life design.

Potato Fougasse

2 cups chopped peeled Yukon gold potatoes or baking potatoes
1 envelope dry yeast ◆ 1 teaspoon brown sugar
1/2 cup warm (100 to 110 degrees) water ◆ 6 cups flour
2 tablespoons olive oil
2 tablespoons chopped fresh rosemary, or 2 teaspoons dried rosemary
1/2 teaspoon salt

Combine the potatoes with enough water to cover in a saucepan. Bring to a boil; reduce the heat. Simmer for 25 minutes or until tender. Drain the potatoes in a colander over a bowl, reserving 1 cup of the cooking liquid. Place the potatoes in a mixing bowl and beat at medium speed until smooth. Dissolve the yeast and brown sugar in 1/2 cup warm water in a mixing bowl. Let stand for 5 minutes. Add 2 cups of the flour, mashed potatoes, reserved cooking liquid, olive oil, rosemary and salt to the yeast mixture. Beat at medium speed until smooth. Stir in 31/2 cups of the flour. Knead the dough on a lightly floured surface for 10 minutes or until smooth and elastic, adding enough of the remaining 1/2 cup flour 1 tablespoon at a time to prevent the dough from sticking to hands. Place the dough in a large bowl sprayed with nonstick cooking spray and turn to coat. Let rise, covered, in a warm place (85 degrees) free from drafts for 45 minutes or until doubled in bulk. Press 2 fingers into the dough. If the indentation remains, the dough has risen enough. Punch the dough down.

Roll the dough into a 10×14-inch rectangle on a baking sheet sprayed with nonstick cooking spray. Imagine a lengthwise line running through the center of the rectangle. Starting at the imaginary line, cut five 4-inch-long diagonal slits in the dough on alternating sides of the line; be careful not to cut through the edge of the dough. Gently pull the slits open. Let rise, covered, for 30 minutes or until doubled in bulk. Bake at 425 degrees for 25 minutes or until light brown. Remove to a wire rack to cool. Cut the loaf lengthwise into halves. Cut each half crosswise into 12 slices.
Yield: 24 (1-slice) servings.

Per Serving:
Calories: 137; Carbohydrate: 26.7 g; Protein: 3.6 g; Total Fat: 1.5 g;
Cholesterol: 0 mg; Sodium: 53 mg; Fiber: 1.1 g;
Calories from Fat: 10%

Breads and Spreads

Rustic Bread

1 envelope dry yeast ◆ 1 teaspoon sugar
1 cup warm (100 to 110 degrees) water
3 1/2 cups all-purpose flour ◆ 1/4 cup whole wheat flour
1/2 cup 1% milk ◆ 2 teaspoons olive oil
1/2 teaspoon salt ◆ 1 tablespoon cornmeal

Dissolve the yeast and sugar in the warm water in a large bowl and mix well. Let stand for 5 minutes. Lightly spoon the flours into dry measuring cups and level with a knife. Add 3 cups of the all-purpose flour, whole wheat flour, 1% milk, olive oil and salt to the yeast mixture and stir with a wooden spoon until smooth. Knead the dough on a lightly floured surface for 10 minutes or until smooth and elastic, adding enough of the remaining 1/2 cup all-purpose flour 1 tablespoon at a time to prevent the dough from sticking to hands; the dough will feel tacky. Place the dough in a large bowl sprayed with nonstick cooking spray and turn to coat. Let rise, covered, in a warm place (85 degrees) free from drafts for 1 hour or until doubled in bulk. Press 2 fingers into the dough. If the indentation remains, the dough has risen enough. Punch the dough down. Let rest, covered, for 5 minutes.

Divide the dough into 2 equal portions. Working with 1 portion at a time and keeping the remaining portion covered to prevent drying out, shape each into a 6-inch oval on a lightly floured surface. Let rise, covered with a damp towel, for 20 minutes; the dough will not double in bulk. Stretch each portion into a 15-inch-long loaf; the loaf will be flat. Arrange the loaves on a baking sheet sprayed with nonstick cooking spray and sprinkled with the cornmeal. Let rise, covered with a damp towel, for 30 minutes; the dough will not double in bulk. Lightly dust each loaf with flour. Bake at 425 degrees for 25 minutes or until the loaves are brown on the bottom and sound hollow when lightly tapped. Remove to a wire rack to cool. **Yield:** 24 (1-slice) servings.

Per Serving:
Calories: 79; Carbohydrate: 15.6 g; Protein: 2.4 g; Total Fat: 0.7 g;
Cholesterol: 0 mg; Sodium: 53 mg; Fiber: 0.7 g;
Calories from Fat: 8%

Breads and Spreads

Pita Chips

3 (6-inch) whole wheat pita rounds, split
1 tablespoon plus 1/2 teaspoon lemon juice
1 garlic clove, crushed
1 tablespoon minced fresh parsley
1 1/2 teaspoons minced fresh chives
1/4 teaspoon salt
1/8 teaspoon pepper

Cut each round into 8 wedges. Arrange the wedges cut side up in a single layer on a large baking sheet. Spray both sides of the wedges with butter-flavor nonstick cooking spray. Combine the lemon juice and garlic in a small bowl and mix well. Brush the tops of the wedges with the lemon juice mixture. Mix the parsley, chives, salt and pepper in a small bowl. Sprinkle the parsley mixture evenly over the wedges. Bake at 350 degrees for 12 minutes or until light brown. Remove to a wire rack to cool completely. Store in an airtight container. **Yield:** 48 (1-chip) servings.

Per Serving:
Calories: 5; Carbohydrate: 1 g; Protein: 0.2 g; Total Fat: 0 g;
Cholesterol: 0 mg; Sodium: 16 mg; Fiber: 0.1 g;
Calories from Fat: 0%

Breads and
Spreads

Lentil Dip with Pita Crisps

Pita Crisps
4 (6-inch) pita rounds, split
1/8 teaspoon salt ♦ 1/8 teaspoon freshly ground pepper

Lentil Dip
1 cup dried small red lentils
1 bay leaf ♦ 1 tablespoon olive oil
1 cup finely chopped onion
2 tablespoons pine nuts ♦ 3 garlic cloves, minced
1 tablespoon tomato paste
1 teaspoon ground coriander seeds
1/2 teaspoon salt ♦ 1/2 teaspoon cumin
1/8 teaspoon red pepper
3 tablespoons fresh lemon juice

For the crisps, cut each round into 5 wedges. Spray 1 side of each pita wedge with garlic-flavor nonstick cooking spray and sprinkle with the salt and pepper. Arrange the wedges in a single layer on a baking sheet. Bake at 350 degrees for 20 minutes or until golden. Remove to a wire rack to cool. Store in an airtight container.

For the dip, sort and rinse the lentils. Combine the lentils and bay leaf in a large saucepan. Add enough water to measure 2 inches above the lentils. Bring to a boil; reduce the heat. Simmer for 8 minutes or until the lentils are tender, stirring occasionally; drain. Discard the bay leaf. Heat the olive oil in a small nonstick skillet over medium-high heat. Sauté the onion and pine nuts in the hot oil for 5 minutes or until light brown. Stir in the garlic, tomato paste, ground coriander, salt, cumin and red pepper. Cook for 5 minutes, stirring occasionally. Stir in the lemon juice. Combine the lentils and onion mixture in a food processor. Process until smooth. Serve with the crisps. **Yield:** 10 (1/4 cup dip and 4 pita crisps) servings.

Per Serving:
Calories: 159; Carbohydrate: 27 g; Protein: 7.4 g; Total Fat: 2.6 g;
Cholesterol: 0 mg; Sodium: 280 mg; Fiber: 3.9 g;
Calories from Fat: 15%

Breads and Spreads

ROASTED GARLIC MAYONNAISE
(AIOLI)

6 to 8 garlic cloves
1 cup fat-free mayonnaise
2 teaspoons fresh lemon juice
1 teaspoon Champagne vinegar
1/8 teaspoon cayenne pepper
1 teaspoon chopped fresh parsley

Wrap the unpeeled garlic cloves in a single layer in a double thickness of foil. Roast at 350 degrees for 45 minutes or until the garlic is soft, turning occasionally. Squeeze the roasted garlic into a food processor or blender, discarding the skins. Add the mayonnaise, lemon juice, vinegar and cayenne pepper. Process until puréed. Spoon the purée into a small serving bowl and stir in the parsley. Store, covered, in the refrigerator for up to 3 days. **Yield:** 16 (1-tablespoon) servings.

PER SERVING:
CALORIES: 12; CARBOHYDRATE: 2.4 g; PROTEIN: 0.1 g; TOTAL FAT: 0 g;
CHOLESTEROL: 0 mg; SODIUM: 105 mg; FIBER: TRACE g;
CALORIES FROM FAT: 0%

BREADS AND
SPREADS

CAPONATA

1 (1-pound) eggplant, cut crosswise into ½-inch slices
2 teaspoons olive oil
½ cup sliced celery
1 cup chopped onion
1 or 2 garlic cloves, minced
1 cup coarsely chopped tomato
3 tablespoons no-salt-added tomato sauce
2 tablespoons red wine vinegar
2 tablespoons chopped black olives
1 tablespoon drained capers
1 teaspoon sugar
¼ teaspoon pepper
⅛ teaspoon salt
1 tablespoon chopped fresh parsley

Arrange the eggplant in a single layer on a baking sheet sprayed with nonstick cooking spray. Brush both sides of the eggplant with the olive oil. Bake at 500 degrees for 8 minutes; turn. Bake for 7 minutes longer. Chop the eggplant and set aside. Spray a large nonstick skillet with nonstick cooking spray and heat over medium heat. Sauté the celery in the hot skillet for 2 minutes. Stir in the onion and garlic. Sauté for 5 minutes. Add the tomato, tomato sauce, vinegar, olives, capers, sugar, pepper and salt to the celery mixture and mix well. Cook over low heat for 10 minutes, stirring frequently. Remove from the heat. Stir in the eggplant and parsley. Spoon into a serving bowl. Chill, covered, for 2 hours. Serve with toasted pita bread wedges or baguette slices.
Yield: 24 (2-tablespoon) servings.

PER SERVING:
CALORIES: 16; CARBOHYDRATE: 2.6 g; PROTEIN: 0.4 g; TOTAL FAT: 0.6 g;
CHOLESTEROL: 0 mg; SODIUM: 56 mg; FIBER: 0.8 g;
CALORIES FROM FAT: 34%

When chopping large amounts of fresh herbs, place a handful in a measuring cup and snip with kitchen scissors. Repeat the process until you've chopped the desired amount.

BREADS AND
SPREADS

BREADS AND SPREADS

OLIVE AND ONION TAPENADE

1 tablespoon olive oil
1 cup chopped onion
4 garlic cloves, finely chopped
2 teaspoons chopped fresh thyme, or 1/2 teaspoon dried thyme
1/4 cup dry white wine
2 tablespoons white wine vinegar
12/3 cups chopped pitted green olives
1/3 cup pitted picholine olives (about 15 olives)
1/4 teaspoon freshly ground pepper

Heat the olive oil in a saucepan over medium heat. Cook the onion in the hot oil for 8 minutes or until tender, stirring frequently. Stir in the garlic and thyme. Cook for 2 minutes, stirring frequently. Add the wine and vinegar and mix well. Bring to a boil; reduce the heat. Cook for 8 minutes or until most of the liquid evaporates, stirring occasionally. Process the onion mixture, olives and pepper in a food processor until smooth, scraping the side of the bowl occasionally. Serve with baguette slices and crudités, such as fennel slices, radishes, celery, carrot sticks and/or red and yellow bell pepper pieces.
Yield: 28 (1-tablespoon) servings.

PER SERVING:
CALORIES: 19; CARBOHYDRATE: 1.1 g; PROTEIN: 0.2 g; TOTAL FAT: 1.7 g;
CHOLESTEROL: 0 mg; SODIUM: 101 mg; FIBER: 0.2 g;
CALORIES FROM FAT: 81%

Mediterranean Tomatoes with Goat Cheese

1 pint grape tomatoes
3 garlic cloves, minced
1 teaspoon olive oil
1 tablespoon minced fresh basil, or 1 teaspoon dried basil
1/8 teaspoon salt
1/8 to 1/4 teaspoon pepper
4 ounces plain or herbed goat cheese

Heat a large nonstick skillet sprayed with garlic-flavor nonstick cooking spray over medium-high heat. Add the tomatoes, garlic and olive oil to the hot skillet. Sauté until the tomatoes are plump and almost ready to burst. Stir in the basil. Remove from the heat. Lightly mash the tomatoes in a bowl just until they burst and season with the salt and pepper. Place the cheese in the center of a warm serving plate and surround the cheese with the tomato mixture. Serve with thinly sliced French baguettes.
Yield: 8 (2-tablespoon) servings.

Per Serving:
Calories: 52; Carbohydrate: 1.9 g; Protein: 3 g; Total Fat: 3.6 g;
Cholesterol: 6.5 mg; Sodium: 91 mg; Fiber: 0.4 g;
Calories from Fat: 62%

Breads and Spreads

DESSERTS

How often have you heard, or thought: "What's for dessert?" Sweets ranging from cakes to pies always seem to find their place at the table after a big meal. Not so in the Mediterranean. People of the Mediterranean countries are accustomed to eating fruit after a meal, as a much healthier alternative.

Fruits contain antioxidants, which help prevent heart disease. Some of the top antioxidant-rich fruits are prunes, raisins, blueberries, strawberries, oranges, grapes, and cherries.

In this region, cakes, pies, and sugary delights are saved for special occasions and eaten in very small portions. Many of the desserts we have included here feature fruits, while others are lighter versions of traditional Mediterranean confections.

Keep turning the pages to sample a few of our favorite Mediterranean delicacies.

BRANDIED APPLES AND PEARS

2 Bosc pears, peeled and cut into quarters
2 Golden Delicious apples, peeled and cut into quarters
2 Rome apples, peeled and cut into quarters
1/4 cup golden raisins
1/4 cup apricot preserves
1/4 cup apple juice
3 tablespoons Calvados (optional)
1 teaspoon cinnamon

Combine the pears, apples, raisins, preserves, apple juice, brandy and cinnamon in a heavy saucepan and mix well. Cook over low heat for 30 minutes or until the fruit is soft, stirring occasionally.
Yield: 4 (1/2-cup) servings.

PER SERVING:
CALORIES: 93; CARBOHYDRATE: 24.4 g; PROTEIN: 0.4 g; TOTAL FAT: 0.4 g;
CHOLESTEROL: 0 mg; SODIUM: 5 mg; FIBER: 2.7 g;
CALORIES FROM FAT: 4%

DESSERTS

MACERATED APRICOTS AND NUTS
(KHOSHAF BIL MISHMISH)

2 cups boiling water
2¹/₂ cups dried apricots
3 tablespoons sugar
¹/₄ cup golden raisins
¹/₄ cup slivered almonds, toasted
2 tablespoons pine nuts, toasted
2 tablespoons chopped pistachios, toasted
1 teaspoon rose water or orange blossom water (optional)

Combine the boiling water and apricots in a medium heatproof bowl. Let stand for 5 minutes. Drain the apricots in a colander over a bowl, reserving the liquid. Combine the reserved liquid, ¹/₂ cup of the apricots and sugar in a blender. Process until puréed. Combine the puréed apricot mixture, remaining apricots, raisins, almonds, pine nuts, pistachios and rose water in a bowl and mix well. Serve chilled or at room temperature.
Yield: 8 (¹/₂-cup) servings.

PER SERVING:
CALORIES: 196; CARBOHYDRATE: 41 g; PROTEIN: 3.6 g; TOTAL FAT: 3.9 g;
CHOLESTEROL: 0 mg; SODIUM: 9 mg; FIBER: 5.5 g;
CALORIES FROM FAT: 18%

Many Middle Eastern puddings and pastries contain rose or orange blossom water. These flavored essences add a distinguishing flavor known only to this region of the Mediterranean. Traditionally, Khoshaf bil Mishmish (pronounced kho-SHAF beel mish-MISH) is eaten to break the daily fast during the Muslim month of Ramadan, but may also be served at the end of a family meal. Rose water and orange blossom water are available at Middle Eastern markets.

DESSERTS

SPICY FRUIT CUP

1 (8-ounce) can juice-pack pineapple chunks
1/2 cup orange juice ◆ 2 tablespoons dry white wine
1/8 teaspoon cinnamon ◆ 1/8 teaspoon nutmeg
Sections of 2 medium oranges
1 medium pear, sliced
1 cup fresh strawberries, cut into halves

Combine the undrained pineapple, orange juice, wine, cinnamon and nutmeg in a bowl and mix gently. Add the orange sections, pear and strawberries to the pineapple mixture and mix gently. Chill, covered, for 1 hour before serving. **Yield:** 6 servings.

PER SERVING:
CALORIES: 78; CARBOHYDRATE: 19 g; PROTEIN: 1 g; TOTAL FAT: 0 g;
CHOLESTEROL: 0 mg; SODIUM: 1 mg; FIBER: 2.6 g;
CALORIES FROM FAT: 0%

STUFFED DATES

24 Medjool dates or other large dates (about 1 pound)
2 drops of green food coloring (optional)
2/3 cup marzipan
2 teaspoons confectioners' sugar

Make a lengthwise slit down the center of each date. Remove the pit if needed. Drizzle the food coloring over the marzipan in a bowl. Gently knead the marzipan 4 or 5 times or until the color is incorporated. Stuff the marzipan into the dates and sprinkle with the confectioners' sugar. **Yield:** 24 (1-date) servings.

PER SERVING:
CALORIES: 50; CARBOHYDRATE: 10.8 g; PROTEIN: 0.6 g; TOTAL FAT: 0.9 g;
CHOLESTEROL: 0 mg; SODIUM: 0 mg; FIBER: 0.6 g;
CALORIES FROM FAT: 17%

DESSERTS

Stuffed Figs with Wine Sauce

12 dried Calimyrna figs
1 cup sweet marsala
1/4 cup orange juice
2 tablespoons sugar
1/3 cup (3 ounces) 1/3-less-fat cream cheese, softened
2 tablespoons freshly grated Parmesan cheese
1 tablespoon chopped pine nuts, toasted
1/2 teaspoon grated orange zest
Orange zest curls (optional)
Sprigs of fresh mint (optional)
Pine nuts (optional)

Combine the figs, wine, orange juice and sugar in a small saucepan and mix well. Bring to a boil and remove from the heat. Let stand, covered, for 15 minutes. Remove the figs to a bowl using a slotted spoon and cover to keep warm, reserving the wine mixture. Bring the reserved wine mixture to a boil. Boil until reduced to 1/4 cup and slightly thickened. Combine the cream cheese, Parmesan cheese, 1 tablespoon pine nuts and 1/2 teaspoon orange zest in a small bowl and mix well. Cut each fig to but not through the stem end. Stuff about 1 1/2 teaspoons of the cheese mixture into the center of each fig. Spoon 1 tablespoon of the wine sauce onto each of 4 dessert plates. Arrange 3 stuffed figs on top of the sauce on each plate. Garnish with orange zest curls, sprigs of mint and pine nuts. **Yield:** 4 servings.

Per Serving:
Calories: 277; Carbohydrate: 50 g; Protein: 5.3 g; Total Fat: 8.3 g;
Cholesterol: 18 mg; Sodium: 132 mg; Fiber: 7.1 g;
Calories from Fat: 27%

Desserts

FRESH PEACH CROUSTADES

¹/4 cup sugar
¹/4 cup water
¹/4 cup small fresh mint leaves
2 cups sliced peeled peaches
1 sheet frozen puff pastry, thawed

Combine the sugar and water in a small saucepan. Bring to a boil. Boil for 1 minute or until the sugar dissolves, stirring occasionally. Let stand until cool. Combine the sugar mixture and mint in a blender. Process until smooth. Combine the mint mixture and peaches in a bowl and mix gently. Cut four 2-inch rounds in the puff pastry using a sharp round cookie cutter. Roll each 2-inch round into a 4-inch round on a lightly floured surface. Arrange the rounds on a baking sheet sprayed with nonstick cooking spray. Bake at 400 degrees for 12 minutes or until golden brown. Top each with ¹/2 cup of the peach mixture.
Yield: 4 (1 croustade and ¹/2 cup peach mixture) servings.

PER SERVING:
CALORIES: 166; CARBOHYDRATE: 28.8 g; PROTEIN: 1.8 g; TOTAL FAT: 5.5 g;
CHOLESTEROL: 0 mg; SODIUM: 37 mg; FIBER: 2.3 g;
CALORIES FROM FAT: 30%

DESSERTS

GRILLED PEACHES WITH RASPBERRY PURÉE

1/2 (10-ounce) package frozen raspberries in light syrup, slightly thawed
1 1/2 teaspoons lemon juice
2 medium peaches, peeled and cut into halves
1 1/2 tablespoons brown sugar
1/4 teaspoon cinnamon
1 1/2 teaspoons rum flavoring
1 1/2 teaspoons margarine

Combine the raspberries and lemon juice in a blender or food processor. Process until puréed. Strain the raspberry purée into a bowl, discarding the seeds. Chill, covered, in the refrigerator. Cut one 18×18-inch sheet of heavy-duty foil. Arrange the peach halves cut side up on the foil. Mix the brown sugar and cinnamon in a bowl and spoon the brown sugar mixture evenly into the centers of the peaches. Drizzle with the flavoring and dot with the margarine. Fold the foil over the peaches and seal loosely. Arrange the foil packet on a grill rack over medium-hot coals. Grill for 15 minutes or until the peaches are heated through. Spoon 2 tablespoons of the raspberry purée over each grilled peach half on a dessert plate. **Yield:** 4 (1 peach half and 2 tablespoons raspberry purée) servings.

PER SERVING:
CALORIES: 99; CARBOHYDRATE: 20 g; PROTEIN: 0.6 g; TOTAL FAT: 1.6 g;
CHOLESTEROL: 0 mg; SODIUM: 19 mg; FIBER: 2.2 g;
CALORIES FROM FAT: 14%

DESSERTS

Listed below are some of the many Italian ice creams available:

Limone—lemon
Fragola—strawberry
Menta—mint
Arancia—orange
Mora di rovo—blackberry
Lampone—raspberry
Yoghurt—yogurt
Caffè—coffee
Mandorla—with slivers of almond
Pistacchio—pistachio
Amaretto—with almond liqueur
Cioccolato—chocolate
Stracciatella—vanilla ice cream with chocolate chips
Vaniglia—vanilla
Amarena—sour cherry
Crema—extra creamy
Nocciola—hazelnut
Albicocca—apricot
Torrone—with nougat, almonds, or Turkish honey

DESSERTS

HONEY-ROASTED PEARS WITH SWEET YOGURT CREAM

Sweet Yogurt Cream
2 cups plain low-fat yogurt
2 tablespoons honey
1/2 teaspoon vanilla extract

Pears
8 firm Bosc pears, cut into quarters
3/4 cup apple cider
1/2 cup honey
1 tablespoon fresh lemon juice
2 teaspoons vanilla extract

For the cream, place a colander in a 2-quart glass measure or medium bowl. Line the colander with 4 layers of cheesecloth, allowing the cheesecloth to extend over the outer edge of the colander. Spoon the yogurt into the colander. Chill, loosely covered with plastic wrap, for 24 hours. Spoon the yogurt cheese into a bowl and discard the liquid. Stir in the honey and vanilla.

For the pears, arrange the pears in a 9×13-inch baking dish sprayed with butter-flavor nonstick cooking spray. Spray the pears with butter-flavor nonstick cooking spray. Combine the cider, honey, lemon juice and vanilla in a small saucepan and mix well. Bring to a boil and pour over the pears. Bake, covered, at 400 degrees for 20 minutes; remove the cover. Bake for 30 minutes longer or until the pears are tender, basting with the pan juices occasionally. Let stand for 10 minutes. Serve warm with the cream. **Yield:** 8 (4 pear quarters, 2 tablespoons basting liquid and 2 tablespoons Sweet Yogurt Cream) servings.

PER SERVING:
CALORIES: 222; CARBOHYDRATE: 52.8 g; PROTEIN: 3.8 g; TOTAL FAT: 1.3 g;
CHOLESTEROL: 2.6 mg; SODIUM: 40 mg; FIBER: 4.1 g;
CALORIES FROM FAT: 5%

POACHED PEARS

1 1/2 cups sparkling grape juice
1 1/2 cups water
1/2 cup sugar
1 sprig of basil or thyme
6 firm ripe pears, such as Bartlett or Bosc

Combine the grape juice, water, sugar and basil in a large saucepan and mix well. Bring to a simmer, stirring occasionally. Peel and core the pears, leaving the stem intact. Arrange the pears stem side up in the simmering syrup as soon as they are peeled. Simmer for 20 to 30 minutes or until cooked through but not mushy. Remove the pears to a platter using a slotted spoon, reserving the syrup. Boil the syrup until reduced to 3/4 of its original volume. Let the pears and syrup cool separately. Drizzle the syrup over the pears and store, covered, in the refrigerator until serving time. For variety, substitute 1 teaspoon cinnamon or 1 cinnamon stick, 3 whole cloves, 1/2 teaspoon nutmeg or 1 teaspoon orange zest for the basil or thyme. **Yield:** 6 servings.

PER SERVING:
CALORIES: 203; CARBOHYDRATE: 52 g; PROTEIN: 0.6 g; TOTAL FAT: 0.7 g;
CHOLESTEROL: 0 mg; SODIUM: 11 mg; FIBER: 4 g;
CALORIES FROM FAT: 3%

DESSERTS

Strawberries with Orange Ricotta Cream

$^1/_2$ cup part-skim ricotta cheese
$^1/_2$ cup vanilla low-fat yogurt
1 tablespoon sugar
$^1/_2$ teaspoon grated orange zest
$^1/_2$ teaspoon vanilla extract
1 cup quartered fresh strawberries
2 whole strawberries (optional)

Combine the cheese, yogurt, sugar, orange zest and vanilla in a blender. Process until smooth. Spoon the cheese mixture into a small bowl. Chill, covered, for 3 hours. Spoon $^1/_2$ cup of the quartered strawberries into each of 2 small bowls. Top each serving with 2 tablespoons of the cheese mixture and garnish with 1 whole strawberry. Store the leftover cheese mixture in the refrigerator for up to 1 week. **Yield:** 2 servings.

PER SERVING:
CALORIES: 76; CARBOHYDRATE: 11.2 g; PROTEIN: 3.7 g; TOTAL FAT: 2.1 g;
CHOLESTEROL: 7 mg; SODIUM: 39 mg; FIBER: 1.7 g;
CALORIES FROM FAT: 25%

DESSERTS

Meringues with Fresh Strawberries and Chocolate Mascarpone ✓

Meringues
2 egg whites ◆ 1/4 teaspoon cream of tartar ◆ 1/2 cup sugar

Chocolate Mascarpone
1 1/2 tablespoons sugar ◆ 1 tablespoon baking cocoa
6 tablespoons (3 ounces) mascarpone cheese, softened
1 to 2 teaspoons fat-free milk ◆ 1/2 teaspoon vanilla extract

Strawberries and Assembly
3 1/2 cups quartered small strawberries (about 1 1/2 quarts)
1/3 cup sugar ◆ Sprigs of fresh mint (optional)

For the meringues, line a baking sheet with baking parchment. Draw six 4-inch circles on the parchment. Turn the parchment over and secure with masking tape. Combine the egg whites and cream of tartar in a mixing bowl. Beat at high speed until foamy. Add the sugar 1 tablespoon at a time, beating constantly until stiff peaks form; do not underbeat. Spread the meringue over the circles using the back of a spoon. Bake at 225 degrees for 1 1/2 hours. Turn the oven off. Let stand with the oven door closed for 30 minutes. Remove the meringues from the parchment to a wire rack to cool. The meringues may be stored in an airtight container for up to 1 week.

For the mascarpone, sift the sugar and baking cocoa together. Combine the cheese, fat-free milk and vanilla in a bowl and stir just until combined. Stir in the baking cocoa mixture.

For the strawberries, toss the strawberries with the sugar in a bowl. Let stand for 15 minutes.

To serve, arrange 1 meringue on each of 6 dessert plates. Spread 1 1/2 tablespoons of the mascarpone on top of each meringue. Top each with 1/2 cup of the strawberries and garnish with sprigs of mint. **Yield:** 6 servings.

Per Serving:
Calories: 211; Carbohydrate: 35.9 g; Protein: 3 g; Total Fat: 7 g;
Cholesterol: 18 mg; Sodium: 28 mg; Fiber: 2.5 g;
Calories from Fat: 30%

Desserts

Flan

1 1/3 cups sugar
3/4 cup egg substitute
1 teaspoon vanilla extract
2 (12-ounce) cans evaporated skim milk

Place 1 cup of the sugar in a large heavy skillet. Cook over medium heat for 5 minutes or until the sugar dissolves; do not stir. Continue cooking until golden brown, stirring constantly. Pour the caramelized sugar into a 9-inch round baking pan, tilting the pan to ensure even coverage over the bottom. Mix the remaining 1/3 cup sugar, egg substitute, vanilla and evaporated skim milk in a bowl. Pour the milk mixture over the prepared layer. Place the round baking pan in a larger baking pan. Add enough hot water to the larger baking pan to measure 1 inch.

Bake at 350 degrees for 1 hour or until a knife inserted near the center comes out clean. Remove the round baking pan to a wire rack to cool completely. Chill, covered, for 4 hours. Loosen the edge of the flan with a knife. Invert onto a serving plate. Drizzle with any remaining syrup and cut into wedges. **Yield:** 8 (1-wedge) servings.

Per Serving:
Calories: 207; Carbohydrate: 43.3 g; Protein: 8.7 g; Total Fat: 0.2 g;
Cholesterol: 3 mg; Sodium: 132 mg; Fiber: 0 g;
Calories from Fat: 1%

Desserts

ITALIAN CUSTARD WITH ROASTED FRUIT
(PANNA COTTA)

2 cups pear nectar
3 envelopes unflavored gelatin
2 cups 1% milk
1 teaspoon vanilla extract
1 cup pitted sweet cherries
4 plums, each cut into 4 wedges
3 peaches, peeled and each cut into 6 wedges
1/4 cup sweet red wine
3 tablespoons honey

Strain the nectar through a fine sieve into a small bowl and discard the solids. Sprinkle the unflavored gelatin over the nectar. Let stand for 1 minute. Combine the 1% milk and gelatin mixture in a medium saucepan and mix well. Cook over medium-low heat until the gelatin dissolves, stirring constantly. Stir in the vanilla. Pour the milk mixture evenly into eight 4-ounce ramekins or muffin cups sprayed with nonstick cooking spray. Chill for 2 hours or until set.

Combine the cherries, plums, peaches, wine and honey in a 9×13-inch baking dish sprayed with nonstick cooking spray and toss to coat. Roast at 400 degrees for 20 minutes or until the fruit is tender, stirring once. Let stand until cool. Loosen the edges of the custards with a sharp knife or rubber spatula. Place a dessert plate upside down over each ramekin and invert the custard onto the plate. Spoon 1/2 cup of the roasted fruit mixture around each custard. **Yield:** 8 servings.

PER SERVING:
CALORIES: 149; CARBOHYDRATE: 30.2 g; PROTEIN: 4.9 g; TOTAL FAT: 1.1 g;
CHOLESTEROL: 2.5 mg; SODIUM: 38 mg; FIBER: 2 g;
CALORIES FROM FAT: 7%

Nonstick cooking spray is an essential item in heart healthy cooking and is used in many of our recipes. We have chosen not to list it as an ingredient at the beginning of the recipe.

DESSERTS

BLUEBERRY PEACH GALETTES

1 (15-ounce) package refrigerated pie pastries
6 cups sliced peeled fresh peaches
1 cup fresh blueberries
1/4 cup sugar
2 tablespoons apricot preserves, melted
1 tablespoon turbinado sugar or granulated sugar

Line a baking sheet with foil or baking parchment. Roll 1 of the pastries into a 12-inch round on a lightly floured surface and arrange on the foil. Combine the peaches, blueberries and 1/4 cup sugar in a bowl and toss to mix. Spread 1/2 of the peach mixture over the pastry round to within 3 inches of the edge. Fold the edge of the pastry toward the center and press gently to seal; the pastry will only partially cover the peach mixture. Brush 1/2 of the preserves over the peach mixture and edge of the pastry. Bake at 425 degrees for 10 minutes. Reduce the oven temperature to 350 degrees. Bake for 20 minutes longer or until light brown. Repeat the procedure with the remaining pastry, remaining peach mixture and remaining preserves. Sprinkle each galette with 1 1/2 teaspoons of the turbinado sugar. Cut each galette into 8 wedges. Serve warm or at room temperature. You may substitute thawed frozen peaches or thawed frozen blueberries for the fresh fruits. **Yield:** 16 (1-wedge) servings.

PER SERVING:
CALORIES: 232; CARBOHYDRATE: 40.6 g; PROTEIN: 2.1 g; TOTAL FAT : 7.6 g;
CHOLESTEROL: 0 mg; SODIUM: 124 mg; FIBER: 2.8 g;
CALORIES FROM FAT: 29%

DESSERTS

CHOCOLATE CHERRY CLAFOUTI

3 cups fresh, frozen or water-pack pitted sweet cherries
1/4 cup miniature chocolate chips
1 cup egg substitute
1 cup 1/2% milk
3/4 cup unbleached flour
1/2 cup sugar
1 tablespoon margarine, melted
1 teaspoon vanilla extract
1/4 teaspoon cinnamon
Confectioners' sugar to taste

Arrange the cherries and chocolate chips in the bottom of a 10-inch baking dish sprayed with butter-flavor nonstick cooking spray. Combine the egg substitute, 1/2% milk, flour, sugar, margarine, vanilla and cinnamon in a blender. Process until smooth. Pour the batter over the cherry mixture. Bake at 350 degrees for 55 to 65 minutes or until the clafouti is puffed and golden brown and a knife inserted in the center comes out clean. Cool for 15 minutes or longer and sprinkle with confectioners' sugar. **Yield**: 8 servings.

PER SERVING:
CALORIES: 197; CARBOHYDRATE: 37.2 g; PROTEIN: 5.7 g; TOTAL FAT: 3.4 g;
CHOLESTEROL: 1.3 mg; SODIUM: 64 mg; FIBER: 0.8 g;
CALORIES FROM FAT: 16%

DESSERTS

Crepes

1¹/2 cups fat-free milk

1 cup flour

1 egg

Raspberry Sauce

1 (12-ounce) package
frozen red raspberries

1 cup sugar

1 teaspoon vanilla extract

CHEESE BLINTZES WITH RASPBERRY SAUCE

Cheese Filling and Assembly

1 cup nonfat cottage cheese ♦ 1 cup low-fat ricotta cheese
1 egg white ♦ 2 tablespoons sugar
1¹/2 teaspoons finely grated orange zest or lemon zest
1 teaspoon vanilla extract ♦ Fresh red raspberries (optional)
Sprigs of mint

For the crepes, combine the fat-free milk, flour and egg in a large mixing bowl. Beat with a rotary beater or at low speed with an electric mixer until blended. Heat a lightly greased 10-inch nonstick skillet over medium heat. Remove from the heat. Spoon a scant ¹/4 cup of the batter into the hot skillet, tilting the skillet to spread the batter evenly over the bottom. Return the skillet to the heat. Cook until brown on 1 side only. Invert the skillet over paper towels to remove. Repeat the process with the remaining batter to make 7 more crepes, greasing the skillet as needed. Chill, covered, until serving time.

For the sauce, combine the raspberries, sugar and vanilla in a medium saucepan and mix well. Cook until thickened and of a syrupy consistency, stirring frequently.

For the filling, combine the cottage cheese, ricotta cheese, egg white, sugar, orange zest and vanilla in a food processor or blender. Process until the mixture is almost smooth. Spread approximately ¹/3 cup of the filling over each crepe to within ¹/2 inch of the edge. Fold the left and right edges to the center and then roll as for a jelly roll. Arrange the crepes seam side down in a baking dish sprayed with nonstick cooking spray. Bake at 400 degrees for 12 to 15 minutes or until heated through. Arrange 1 blintz on each of 8 dessert plates and drizzle with 2 tablespoons of the sauce. Garnish with fresh raspberries and sprigs of mint. **Yield:** 8 (1 blintz and 2 tablespoons sauce) servings.

PER SERVING:
CALORIES: 230; CARBOHYDRATE: 35.6 g; PROTEIN: 12 g; TOTAL FAT: 3.3 g;
CHOLESTEROL: 39.4 mg; SODIUM: 170 mg; FIBER: 0.8 g;
CALORIES FROM FAT: 13%

Phyllo Crisps with Nectarines and Pears

2½ cups chopped nectarines or apricots
2 cups chopped Bartlett or Anjou pears
¼ cup sugar ◆ ¼ cup packed brown sugar
2 (3-inch) cinnamon sticks ◆ 1 teaspoon vanilla extract
3 sheets frozen phyllo pastry, thawed
6 tablespoons confectioners' sugar ◆ ¼ cup ground walnuts
½ cup fat-free caramel ice cream sauce

Combine the nectarines, pears, sugar, brown sugar and cinnamon sticks in a large saucepan and mix well. Bring to a boil; reduce the heat. Simmer for 35 minutes or until most of the liquid evaporates, stirring occasionally. Stir in the vanilla. Let stand until cool. Discard the cinnamon sticks. Line a large baking sheet with baking parchment. Arrange 1 of the pastry sheets on the baking parchment and spray with butter-flavor nonstick cooking spray. Sprinkle with 2 tablespoons of the confectioners' sugar and 4 teaspoons of the walnuts. Repeat the layers twice with the remaining 2 pastry sheets, remaining confectioners' sugar and remaining walnuts, spraying each pastry sheet with butter-flavor nonstick cooking spray. Using a sharp knife or pizza cutter, cut the stacked pastries into twenty-four 2½×3-inch rectangles. Cover the rectangles with baking parchment.

Coat the bottom of another baking sheet with butter-flavor nonstick cooking spray and arrange the baking sheet coated side down over the rectangles. Bake at 350 degrees for 12 minutes or until golden brown. Remove the top baking sheet and baking parchment carefully. Cool the phyllo crisps on a wire rack. To serve, arrange 1 phyllo crisp on each of 8 dessert plates. Top each crisp with 1½ tablespoons of the fruit compote. Repeat the layers with the remaining phyllo crisps and remaining fruit compote, ending with the phyllo crisps. Drizzle each serving with 1 tablespoon caramel sauce. **Yield:** 8 servings.

Per Serving:
Calories: 226; Carbohydrate: 49.7 g; Protein: 2.6 g; Total Fat: 4.3 g;
Cholesterol: 0 mg; Sodium: 72 mg; Fiber: 2.3 g;
Calories from Fat: 17%

Phyllo may be stored in the refrigerator for up to one month or frozen for up to one year. If frozen, thaw the dough completely in the refrigerator before using. Remove the phyllo from the refrigerator two hours prior to handling for the best results. Refreezing thawed phyllo is not recommended because the dough becomes crumbly, dry, and hard to work with.

Desserts

√

QUICK AND EASY TIRAMISU

6 cups (1-inch) cubes angel food cake, about 1 (10-inch) cake
2 packages vanilla instant cappuccino mix, such as Maxwell House
1 cup hot water
8 ounces Neufchâtel cheese
1/2 cup packed brown sugar
1 teaspoon vanilla extract
1/2 teaspoon cinnamon
8 ounces frozen reduced-calorie whipped topping
1 tablespoon baking cocoa

Arrange the cake cubes in a single layer in a 9×13-inch baking dish. Combine the cappuccino mix and hot water in a small bowl and mix well. Pour the cappuccino over the cake cubes. Combine the cheese, brown sugar, vanilla and cinnamon in a large mixing bowl. Beat at high speed for 2 minutes or until fluffy, scraping the bowl occasionally. Fold the whipped topping into the cheese mixture. Spread the cheese mixture over the cake cubes. Sift the baking cocoa over the top of the prepared layers. Chill, covered, for 1 hour. **Yield:** 12 (3-inch squares) servings.

PER SERVING:
CALORIES: 218; CARBOHYDRATE: 34.7 g; PROTEIN: 4.4 g; TOTAL FAT: 7.3 g;
CHOLESTEROL: 15 mg; SODIUM: 223 mg; FIBER: 1.7 g;
CALORIES FROM FAT: 30%

DESSERTS

EGYPTIAN ORANGE CAKE

Cake
1 cup cake flour
1 tablespoon baking powder
1/2 teaspoon baking soda
1/8 teaspoon salt
1/2 cup sugar
1 cup fresh orange juice
1 teaspoon vanilla extract or flavoring of choice

Orange Glaze
1/2 cup fresh orange juice
1/2 cup sugar

For the cake, sift the cake flour, baking powder, baking soda and salt into a bowl and mix well. Stir in the sugar. Add the orange juice and vanilla and whisk until blended. Spoon the batter into a 9-inch cake pan sprayed with nonstick cooking spray. Bake at 350 degrees for 25 to 35 minutes or until the cake tests done. Cool in the pan on a wire rack for 10 minutes. Invert onto a cake plate.

For the glaze, combine the orange juice and sugar in a small saucepan. Bring to a boil. Cook until a candy thermometer registers 220 degrees or until the sugar caramelizes and the mixture is of a syrupy consistency, stirring constantly. Drizzle the glaze over the top of the warm cake. Let stand until cool before slicing. **Yield:** 12 servings.

PER SERVING:
CALORIES: 112; CARBOHYDRATE: 27 g; PROTEIN: 1 g; TOTAL FAT: 0.2 g;
CHOLESTEROL: 0 mg; SODIUM: 182 mg; FIBER: 0.2 g;
CALORIES FROM FAT: 2%

Egyptians traditionally serve Egyptian Orange Cake to end the fasting during the Muslim month of Ramadan.

DESSERTS

ALMOND MACAROONS

2 tablespoons matzo cake meal
3/4 cup blanched whole almonds
3/4 cup matzo cake meal
3/4 cup sugar
1/2 cup chopped dried apricots
3 egg whites
1 teaspoon grated orange zest
1/4 teaspoon almond extract

Line a cookie sheet with baking parchment and sprinkle 2 tablespoons matzo cake meal over the parchment. Place the almonds in a food processor and pulse 3 or 4 times or just until coarsely chopped. Lightly spoon 3/4 cup matzo cake meal into a dry measuring cup and level with a knife. Add 3/4 cup matzo cake meal, sugar, apricots, egg whites, orange zest and flavoring to the almonds. Pulse 3 or 4 times or just until combined; the mixture will be sticky.

Using hands dusted with matzo cake meal, divide the dough into 16 equal portions. Roll each portion into a ball and pinch the top of each ball to form a pear shape. Arrange 2 inches apart on the prepared cookie sheet. Bake at 325 degrees for 20 minutes or until light brown. Cool on the cookie sheet for 2 minutes. Remove to a wire rack to cool completely. Store in an airtight container. **Yield:** 16 (1-macaroon) servings.

PER SERVING:
CALORIES: 117; CARBOHYDRATE: 19.8 g; PROTEIN: 3 g; TOTAL FAT: 3.5 g;
CHOLESTEROL: 0 mg; SODIUM: 13 mg; FIBER: 1.4 g;
CALORIES FROM FAT: 27%

DESSERTS

Strawberry Gelato

2 cups sugar ◆ 2 cups water
5 cups quartered fresh strawberries (about 4 pints) ◆ 2 cups buttermilk

Bring the sugar and water to a boil in a large saucepan. Boil until the sugar dissolves, stirring constantly. Pour the sugar syrup into a large heatproof bowl. Let stand until cool. Process the strawberries in a blender until puréed. Stir the strawberry purée and buttermilk into the sugar syrup. Add the strawberry mixture to an ice cream freezer container. Freeze using manufacturer's directions. **Yield**: 8 (1/2-cup) servings.

PER SERVING:
CALORIES: 134; CARBOHYDRATE: 31.7 g; PROTEIN: 1.6 g; TOTAL FAT: 0.8 g;
CHOLESTEROL: 1 mg; SODIUM: 17 mg; FIBER: 1.7 g;
CALORIES FROM FAT: 5%

Strawberry Orange Granita

1 cup water ◆ 1/2 cup sugar
1 cup fresh or frozen strawberries ◆ 1 1/2 cups orange juice
1 teaspoon freshly grated lemon zest ◆ Sprigs of mint (optional)

Combine the water and sugar in a small saucepan. Cook over medium heat until the sugar dissolves, stirring constantly. Stir in the strawberries. Cook for 2 minutes or until the strawberries are soft, stirring frequently. Process the mixture in a food mill or press through a fine sieve, discarding the solids. Combine the strawberry purée, orange juice and lemon zest in a freezer-safe container and mix well. Freeze, covered, until firm. Serve by scraping the mixture with a metal spoon or ice cream scoop into tall Champagne glasses or martini glasses. Garnish with sprigs of mint. **Yield:** 6 (1/2-cup) servings.

PER SERVING:
CALORIES: 100; CARBOHYDRATE: 24.8 g; PROTEIN: 0.6 g; TOTAL FAT: 0.2 g;
CHOLESTEROL: 0 mg; SODIUM: 0.8 mg; FIBER: 0.7 g;
CALORIES FROM FAT: 2%

Gelato refers to any type of ice cream made from a basic recipe of milk, sugar, and egg yolk. The individual flavors are achieved by adding various flavorings. Granita is a drink made with fruit juice, syrup, or black coffee poured over crushed ice.

DESSERTS

Lemon Basil Sorbet

3 cups loosely packed fresh basil leaves, torn
1¹/2 cups sugar
1¹/2 cups water
¹/2 cup light corn syrup
2 cups fresh lemon juice (about 2 pounds lemons)

Combine the basil, sugar, water and corn syrup in a saucepan and mix well. Bring to a boil. Boil for 3 minutes or until the sugar dissolves, stirring frequently. Remove from the heat and chill. Strain the basil mixture through a sieve into a bowl, pressing the basil with the back of a spoon to remove as much liquid as possible; discard the basil. Combine the basil mixture and lemon juice in a bowl and mix well. Pour the basil mixture into an ice cream freezer container. Freeze using manufacturer's directions. Spoon the sorbet into a freezer-safe container. Freeze, covered, for 1 hour or until firm. Let stand at room temperature for 10 minutes before serving. **Yield:** 10 (¹/2-cup) servings.

Per Serving:
Calories: 175; Carbohydrate: 46.7 g; Protein: 0.2 g; Total Fat: 0 g;
Cholesterol: 0 mg; Sodium: 21 mg; Fiber: 0.2 g;
Calories from Fat: 0%

Desserts

Orange Juice Sorbet

1 quart fresh orange juice
2 tablespoons Cointreau or other orange liqueur (optional)
1/4 teaspoon lemon extract
Sliced fresh strawberries (optional)

Combine the orange juice, liqueur and flavoring in an ice cream freezer container and mix well. Freeze using manufacturer's directions. Spoon into dessert goblets and serve with sliced strawberries. If an ice cream freezer is not available, pour the orange juice mixture into 3 large ice cube trays. Freeze for 8 to 10 hours or until firm. Let stand at room temperature for 5 to 10 minutes or until the cubes begin to thaw and soften. Process the slightly thawed cubes in a blender or food processor until smooth. Serve immediately in dessert goblets with strawberries. The leftovers may be refrozen and reblended in a food processor as needed. The sorbet texture actually becomes smoother with a second freezing and second blending. **Yield:** 8 (1/2-cup) servings.

Per Serving:
Calories: 69; Carbohydrate: 14.5 g; Protein: 0.9 g; Total Fat: 0.3 g;
Cholesterol: 0 mg; Sodium: 1.5 mg; Fiber: 0.3 g;
Calories from Fat: 4%

Milk or eggs are not used in the preparation of sorbet. This low-calorie dessert is a water-based ice made from fruit juice, fruit purée, buts of fruit, syrup, wine, spirits, sugar, or other flavoring ingredients.

Desserts

Appendix

We hope you have enjoyed learning more about the Mediterranean way of life. In this section, we have included nutritional profile guidelines, so you can make better choices for your own cardiovascular health.

The glossary that follows is a quick reference to ingredients and dishes that may not be familiar. Fortunately, large supermarkets and small neighborhood groceries alike are broadening their selections, making it simpler for you to find the food items you need for these recipes.

From everyone at the Saint Thomas Heart Institute, we wish you the best on your journey to the "heart" of the Mediterranean.

Acknowledgments

Marjorie Clements

Beth Collins, Executive Chef

Bill Crawford

Jeanne Dalton

Amy Ewing

Jim Finley

Luis Garcia

Tara Geske

Gerry Hagan

R. Harold Hipps

Aubrey Knott

Sandy Maxwell

Mary Margaret O'Connor

Joyce Palevo

Randy Pendergrass

Emily Stephenson

NUTRITIONAL PROFILE GUIDELINES

The recipes in this cookbook were analyzed by a registered dietitian. This cookbook is for any individual wishing to make lifestyle changes to reduce the risk of heart disease. The collection of recipes has been modified to reduce total fat, saturated fat, cholesterol, and sodium. Persons who have diabetes mellitus may use these recipes if they are using the carbohydrate counting method of the American Diabetic Association exchange system; however, recipes containing excessive simple carbohydrates and sugars are not suitable. References used for analysis include *Bowes and Church's Food Values of Portions Commonly Used,* by Jean A. T. Pennington, 17th edition, and available nutrition information from newly released food products. Most of the recipes meet the dietary guidelines of the American Heart Association and the National Cholesterol Education Program; however, some of the recipes, even though they have been modified, still contain more than 30% fat. Further reduction in fat would jeopardize the traditional characteristics and flavor of the recipes. These foods when eaten in moderation with other foods that are low in fat can provide an average intake of 30% or less calories from fat, less than 10% calories from saturated fat, 300 mg or less cholesterol, and sodium under 3000 mg per day. Persons with dietary or health problems, whose diets require close monitoring, should consult their physician or registered dietitian for specific information.

♦ Alcoholic ingredients have been analyzed for the basic ingredients, although cooking causes the evaporation of alcohol, thus decreasing caloric content.

♦ Buttermilk, sour cream, and yogurt are the types available commercially which contain 1% milkfat or less.

♦ Cottage cheese is 1% milkfat or nonfat.

♦ Cheese is reduced-fat containing 5 grams fat or less per one-ounce portion, or fat-free.

♦ Milk is 1% milkfat, ½% milkfat or skim. Evaporated milk is skimmed evaporated milk, and sweetened condensed milk is the fat-free type.

♦ Flour is unsifted all-purpose unless the recipe specifies unbleached, self-rising, whole wheat, etc.

♦ Margarine is the type containing liquid oil as its first ingredient.

♦ Oil is olive oil unless specified otherwise.

♦ Chicken, cooked for boning and chopping, has been roasted; this method yields the lowest caloric value.

♦ Egg white is the white of 1 large egg, and eggs when used are large. Cholesterol-free egg substitutes are the varieties with ¼ cup equivalent to 1 egg.

♦ Salt and other ingredients to taste as noted in the ingredients have not been included in the nutritional profile.

♦ Garnishes, serving suggestions, and other optional additions and variations are not included in the profile.

♦ If a choice of ingredients has been given, the nutritional profile information reflects the first option. If a choice of amounts has been given, the nutritional profile reflects the greater amount.

NUTRITIONAL PROFILE GUIDELINES

GLOSSARY

Aïoli—A garlic-infused mayonnaise.

Almond paste—Made from ground blanched almonds, sugar, and a little glycerine to keep it malleable. Sweeter and coarser than marzipan. Used mainly for pastries.

Amaretto—An almond-flavored liqueur.

Asiago cheese—A semifirm Italian cheese with a rich, nutty flavor. It's made from whole or part-skim cow's milk and comes in small wheels with glossy rinds. The yellow interior has many small holes. Young asiago is used as a table cheese. After it has been aged over a year, it becomes hard and suitable for grating.

Avgolemono—Egg and lemon mixture used in Greek cooking.

Baba ghanouj—Roasted eggplant salad or dip.

Baklava—Greek pastry made of layers of flaky dough with ground nuts and honey.

Balsamic vinegar—A thick, strong, slightly sweet aged vinegar imported from Italy.

Bouquet garni—A tied bundle of herbs and other seasonings that is added to soups, stews, and other dishes for flavoring and removed after cooking.

Broccoli rabe—A cross between a turnip green and broccoli. It has long leafy stems with tiny broccoli flowers. The flavor is closer to that of greens than broccoli.

Bruschetta—Thick slices of bread toasted on both sides. They are rubbed with a cut clove of garlic and drizzled with olive oil.

Bulgur—Hulled wheat that has been steamed until partially cooked, then dried and ground. Sold in fine, medium, and coarse grinds.

Capers—These are pickled buds from a Mediterranean bush. The buds are cleaned and sun-dried before being preserved in brine. They take about one month to cure and can be stored for about one year. Rinse off brine before using.

Caponata—A dish composed of eggplant, onions, tomatoes, anchovies, olives, pine nuts, capers, and vinegar, cooked together in olive oil. It's most often served at room temperature.

Chorizo—Spanish cured pork sausage heavily flavored with paprika and garlic. Spanish versions are mild, while Latin American versions are hot.

Christopsomo—"Christ bread," the special bread that is a central part of the Greek Christmas dinner and celebrations.

Clafouti—A country French dessert made by topping a layer of fresh fruit with batter. After baking it's served hot, sometimes with cream. Some clafoutis have a cakelike topping, while others are more like a pudding.

Clarified butter—Unsalted butter that has been slowly melted to separate the milk solids. The white foam is skimmed off the top, and the golden, clear liquid is carefully poured off into another container. The milk solids on the pan bottom ar then discarded. Clarified butter has a higher smoking point than regular butter.

Couscous—Staple starch of North African cuisine. Couscous is tiny pasta-like pellets made from semolina flour and salted water, usually cooked by steaming.

Crostini—Originally crostini were thick little crusts of stale bread dipped briefly in wine or broth or salted water to refresh them. Today, crostini usually refers to appetizers that use thick slices of bread as the base.

Croustade—An edible container or crisp base made from pastry or bread and used to hold fruit, stew, or a vegetable mixture. Depending on the filling, a croustade may be used as an appetizer, main dish, or dessert.

Cumin—Tiny, yellow-brown seeds with a pungent, spicy taste. Commonly available already ground. However, for the fullest flavor, it is best to grind them just before using.

Currants—Tiny, dried raisin-like fruits originally from Corinth. They add an intense sweet flavor to desserts and are also used in several southern Italian pasta and vegetable dishes.

Ditalini—A very small tube-shaped macaroni.

Fattoush—A Lebanese toasted bread salad.

Fava bean—Also known as broad bean. When very young, the whole beans, pods and all, are eaten. When mature, the fresh beans are shelled. A tough skin on the beans themselves should be removed before cooking. Dried favas range in color from green to purplish brown. They are commonly available already peeled.

Feta cheese—A soft, crumbly white Greek cheese made from goat or sheep's milk. Firmer fetas are made from cow's milk and can be used in salads or appetizers.

Fontina cheese—A semifirm cow's milk cheese with about 45 percent milk fat. It melts easily and smoothly due to the high milk fat content. It has a dark golden brown rind with a pale yellow interior dotted with tiny holes.

Galette—A rustic tart or pie made with pastry dough or yeast dough. During assembly, the filling is placed in the center of the rolled-out circle of dough, leaving a three-inch border. The edges of the dough are folded toward the center of the tart, only partially covering the filling.

Haloumi—Salty sheep's milk cheese with a string-like consistency. Made in Cyprus, where it is flavored with mint, and in Lebanon, where black cumin is added.

Harissa—North African hot sauce made from chili pepper and cumin. A tiny dot of the sauce is usually enough to season a serving of couscous. It is sometimes found in cans or in tubes in the specialty foods section of supermarkets, and in Middle Eastern markets.

Hazelnut—Also called filberts. Rich-flavored pale yellow nut covered by brown skin and a hard shell. To remove the skins, shell the nuts and then toast in a 350-degree Fahrenheit oven for 7 to 10 minutes, or until the skin begins to flake, then wrap in a kitchen towel and rub vigorously while the nut is warm to remove as much of the skin as possible.

Macerate—A process of soaking fruit in a liquid in order to infuse it with the liquid's flavor. Often a spirit such as brandy, rum, or a liqueur is used as the macerating liquid.

Marsala—A wine produced in the town of Marsala and neighboring towns in western Sicily. Marsala can be sweet or dry and is about 18 percent alcohol.

Mascarpone cheese—A buttery-rich double-cream to triple-cream cheese made from cow's milk. It is ivory colored with a texture of room-temperature butter.

Mozzarella cheese—A rindless, white southern Italian cheese traditionally made from the milk of the water buffalo, but now commonly made from cow's milk.

GLOSSARY

Olives—Green and black cured olives are popular throughout the Mediterranean. There are many different varieties and ways to flavor them. Among the most common types are niçoise, small brownish-black Provençal brine-cured olives packed in olive oil; Kalamata, brine-cured black Greek olives packed in vinegar; Gaeta, small salt-cured black Italian olives; and dark-green cracked olives popular in Provence and Greece.

Olive oil—Olive oil is labeled according to different grades, which are based on acidity. The best olive oils are called extra-virgin, first cold pressing. Other grades include superfine, fine, virgin, and pure. Pressings after the first cold pressing may use heat or chemicals to help extract the oil.

Orange flower water—A fragrant, intensely flavored liquid distilled from orange blossoms used for making pastries. It is available at stores that specialize in Middle Eastern foods.

Orange zest—A strip of orange zest from an orange peel, with the bitter white part cut away. Zest is used for flavoring dishes or sprinkled on top as a colorful garnish.

Paella—A Spanish dish of rice cooked with onion, tomato, garlic, saffron, vegetables, and various meats, including chicken, chorizo, and/or shellfish.

Pancetta—Italian cured pig belly, the same cut used to make bacon. Most often rolled into a sausage-like shape, but sometimes available flat. Flavored with cloves and black pepper, it is cured for at least 20 days. Occasionally available smoked.

Panzanella—An Italian bread salad.

Parmesan cheese—Hard, dry cheese made from skimmed or partially skimmed cow's milk. It has a hard, golden rind and straw-colored interior with a rich, sharp flavor. The best Parmesan is Parmigiano-Reggiano, produced in the areas of Bologna, Mantua, Modena, or Parma. It is aged for over two years and has a granular texture. The flavor and texture is best when freshly grated.

Pesto—A sauce consisting of basil, garlic, olive oil, and Parmesan cheese. High in fat; use small amounts.

Phyllo dough—Sometimes spelled filo. This is a paper-thin Greek pastry dough, usually found in the frozen foods section of the supermarket.

Pine nut—The long, thin nut of the stone pine tree. These are also known as pignoli. Used in many dishes, both sweet and savory, throughout the Mediterranean. An Asian variety is sometimes stronger in flavor and not as desirable for use in Mediterranean dishes.

Polenta—A mush made from cornmeal. It can be eaten hot like grits or cooled until firm, cut into squares, and grilled or fried.

Pomegranate juice and seeds—Pomegranates keep well for months in a cool, dry place if not picked too ripe. The sweet-tart juice extracted from its seeds is used for syrups, sherbets, and in drinks. The juice is also available in bottles in Middle Eastern shops. The seeds also are used as a garnish for soups and puddings.

Porcini—Large, wild mushrooms prized for their meaty texture and woody flavor. When fresh, they are commonly grilled whole or sliced and sautéed. They are also available dried.

Prosciutto—Raw salt-cured ham that has been aged to produce moist, lightly veined, intense pink meat with an edge of fat.

GLOSSARY

Provolone cheese—Southern Italian cheese made with cow's milk. Available in a variety of shapes and sizes. Young provolone is sweet, while strong provolone has been aged for up to one year. Available smoked as well.

Pulses—Another name for lentils, peas, and beans. .

Quinoa—A tiny, bead-shaped grain introduced by the Incas containing more protein than any other grain. The ivory-colored quinoa cooks in half the time that rice requires and expands to four times its original volume.

Ricotta cheese—The name means "recooked." The cheese is made by heating the whey of another cooked cheese like mozzarella or provolone. It is a soft, white, mildly sweet, and creamy cheese. It is used in desserts and in fillings for stuffed pastas.

Romano cheese—There are several different styles of Romano cheese, all of which take their name from the city of Rome. Pecorino Romano is a sharp, tangy cheese made with sheep's milk. Caprino Romano is an extremely sharp goat's milk cheese. Vacchino Romano is a very mild cow's milk cheese. The pale yellow Romano is very firm and mostly used for grating.

Rose water—Distilled from fragrant rose petals used as flavoring for desserts and syrups.

Saffron—These are the golden yellow stamens of a purple crocus flower. This very expensive spice is mostly grown in Spain. Cheap imitations are often crushed marigold petals or turmeric.

Semolina—A hard-wheat flour made from durum wheat; prized for pasta making because it produces a dough that cooks up firmly.

Sumac—Crushed dried red berries of a species of nonpoisonous sumac shrub. It has a sour, somewhat lemony taste with a hint of pepper. Whole and ground berries are available in Middle Eastern stores.

Tagine—Name for a Moroccan terra-cotta cooking utensil and the stew cooked in it.

Tahini—A thick, oily paste of ground sesame seeds used in Middle Eastern cooking. Tahini separates upon standing and requires stirring before using. Refrigerate after opening to prevent rancidity.

Tapenade—A thick paste made from capers, anchovies, ripe olives, olive oil, lemon juice, seasonings and sometimes small pieces of tuna. It's used as a condiment and served with crudités or bread crisps.

Truffle—This is a variety of fungus known for its unusual smell. Because of its unique smell, truffle hunters can use certain breeds of pigs and dogs to sniff them out. The truffles grow underground near the roots of oak, willow, and hazelnut trees. They are highly sought after and quite expensive.

Turmeric—A rhizome that yields a yellowish-orange powder when dried and ground. It is often combined with saffron to enhance the color of Moroccan dishes.

Yogurt—In the Middle East yogurt is made every day. Varieties of yogurt from whole milk to nonfat are available in stores. Recipes may specify drained, thickened yogurt. To drain, place in a sieve lined with cheesecloth in the refrigerator and let drain from three hours to overnight. It will thicken and become like a soft cheese.

Wheat berries—The whole grain from which flour is ground. They can be found in the natural foods section of the grocery store or at a natural foods market.

GLOSSARY

Index

INDEX

INDEX

INDEX